TERRACIDE

TERRACIDE HUBERT REEVES

Translated by Donald Winkler

Cormorant Books

Canada Council for the Arts | Conseil des Arts du Canada

The publisher gratefully acknowledges the support of the Canada Council for the Arts and the Ontario Arts Council for its publishing program. We acknowledge the financial support of the Government of Canada through the Book Publishing Industry Development Program (BPIDP) for our publishing activities.

Printed and bound in Canada

LIBRARY AND ARCHIVES CANADA CATALOGUING IN PUBLICATION

Reeves, Hubert, 1932–
Terracide / Hubert Reeves ; translated by Donald Winkler.

Translation of: Mal de terre.
Interviews by Frédéric Lenoir.
Includes bibliographical references.
ISBN 978-1-897151-00-6

1. Global environmental change. 2. Environmental degradation. 3. Environmental protection. 4. Reeves, Hubert, 1932– — Interviews. I. Lenoir, Frédéric II. Winkler, Donald III. Title.

GE149.R4413 2009 333.7 C2006-901862-6
Cover design: Angel Guerra/Archetype
Text design: Tannice Goddard, Soul Oasis Networking
Printer: Imprimerie Gauvin

CORMORANT BOOKS INC.
215 SPADINA AVENUE, STUDIO 230, TORONTO, ONTARIO, CANADA M5T 2C7
www.cormorantbooks.com

Mixed Sources
Product group from well-managed forests and recycled wood or fiber
www.fsc.org Cert no. SGS-COC-2624
© 1996 Forest Stewardship Council

This book is dedicated to
Camille Scoffier-Reeves, my wife,
with enormous gratitude for her expert assistance
and her invaluable contribution to
my writings over the last twenty-five years.

PREFACE

THIS BOOK WAS FIRST WRITTEN and published in French under the name *Mal de Terre* in 2003. It sold over fifty thousand copies in France, Belgium, Switzerland, and Canada. In 2005, revisions were made, and up-to-date information was added. Due to complicated circumstances, it has taken longer than was hoped for this English translation to appear. For this reason, I went back through the text again and made a later revision in 2008. The text is up-to-date but some of the figures (graphs) are lacking the most recent information. As well, the bibliography does not contain all of the most recent books and articles on this subject.

CONTENTS

TERRACIDE

PROLOGUE

The Future of Life on Earth

The challenge we face is none other than ensuring humanity's survival.
MIKHAIL GORBACHEV

I HAVE OFTEN BEEN ASKED why, as an astrophysicist accustomed to describing the stars and galaxies, I have undertaken to write a book about the state of our planet.

The reason is that, beyond being a researcher in astrophysics, I live on the Earth, and I am a citizen of this world. I also have children, grandchildren, and friends who are dear to me. Our future on this planet is a matter of great concern. It took billions of years for life on Earth to produce the marvel that is the human brain. It's a fabulous cosmic odyssey that could very well founder by our own fault.

The litany of ecological disasters and threats to our biosphere is well documented, and we will be returning to it throughout this book. The list includes global warming; the thinning of the ozone layer; soil, air, and water pollution; the depletion of natural resources; the disappearance of forests and wetlands; the accelerated extinction of living species; and the insane accumulation of chemical and nuclear waste. Our planet is in bad shape.

History provides us with a long line of Cassandras and prophets of doom. The reader may very well ask: do the cries of alarm being raised today come from false prophets as well?

It is important, so as not to be confused with those harbingers of the apocalypse, that we stick closely to established facts, and monitor as accurately as possible the truth of what we say. The scientist's duty is to assess with a critical cast of mind the seriousness of the dangers facing us, and to be extremely cautious in presenting results and evidence for conclusions.

I will make much of what has been called the "precautionary principle."[1] Must we, in fact, wait for complete and irrefutable proof of danger before taking it seriously? If you see smoke in your kitchen, you are alarmed before you know for certain there is a fire.

Incidentally, we can confirm that alarmist predictions in the past, even when shown to be exaggerated, have often played a useful role. Advanced warnings have done much to reduce the scale of impending catastrophes.[2]

It's important to distinguish the fate of humanity from that of life as a whole. Life, we now know, is extraordinarily resilient. It will continue to adapt and to flourish as it has done for the last billion years in an astonishing variety of forms. But we humans are much more fragile. Our survival depends upon the future conditions of the planet's surface.

We are capable of making the planet unlivable for our descendants. We have embarked on a perilous experiment with our climate on a planetary scale. The effects are already visible, and we are monitoring those to come with some anxiety. No one can foresee when this experiment will stop, or what the biosphere will look like when it does.

Unlike a scientific researcher, we cannot simply stop the experiment midway if it turns bad. Nor can we close up the laboratory and go home. We are in the test tube, along with our children and grandchildren.

THE HUMAN CATACLYSM

A revealing comparison can be made between the current situation and the biological crisis that took place sixty-five million years ago.

At that time, a giant meteorite struck the Earth in Yucatán, a state in Mexico. The consequences of that collision were cataclysmic. The shock generated energy comparable to that of hundreds of millions of atomic bombs. There are excellent reasons to believe that this impact was responsible for the disappearance of the great saurians (such as the famous dinosaurs) as well as 50% of all living species.[3] The phenomenon was short-lived: a few seconds for the shock, a few decades of climatic and biological fallout. Happily for us, our distant ancestors, small tree-dwelling monkeys that one can find today in Madagascar, survived the catastrophe. Subsequently, radical changes took place in the evolution of life. Mammals, which had already existed for more than a hundred million years, proliferated enormously, bringing into the world primates, hominids, and Homo sapiens (ourselves).

Geologists call the period that preceded this event "the Cretaceous," and the period that followed, "the Tertiary." This chronological distinction derives from the discrepancies in the fossil record before and after that date. Geologists have identified five great episodes of biological extinction in the Earth's history, the most recent being that of the dinosaurs.[4]

Today, we are experiencing upheavals that risk being as grave as those in geological ages past. Which is why the term "sixth extinction" has been applied to the current crisis. This term, alas, seems perfectly justified. At the Bonn Convention on Biological Diversity (May 2008), experts estimated that the annual rate of species extinction today is a thousand times more rapid than before the industrial era, and that more than 30% of all species could disappear by 2050, with no guarantee that the trend will stop there. (See below, "Estimates of the rate and extent of the extinction of living species.")

The current crisis has many causes, and almost all of them relate more or less directly to human activity. These will be enumerated throughout the course of the book.

ESTIMATES OF THE RATE AND EXTENT OF THE EXTINCTION OF LIVING SPECIES

Robert May of Oxford University and President of the Royal Society, in a speech in November 2001 at the annual conference of the Society for Conservation Biology: "The rate of species extinction has accelerated over the last hundred years, to about a thousand times what it was before the arrival of humans."

E. O. Wilson, Harvard University (one of the most distinguished biologists of our time), in The Diversity of Life: "We estimate today that between 1 and 10% of species are eliminated each decade, or about 27,000 each year."

Michael Novacek, the American Museum of Natural History in New York: "It is not unrealistic to foresee that we will have exterminated half of all living species by the middle of the twenty-first century."

A 1998 survey indicated that 70% of biologists believe that we are in the middle of a massive wave of extinction. A third expect a 10 to 50% loss of species over the next thirty years.

According to the United Nations Environment Programme, close to 25% of mammals (1,130 species) and 12% of bird species are threatened with extinction.

SOURCE: SCIENTIFIC AMERICAN, NOVEMBER 2001.

VISIBLE SIGNS OF WARMING

One of the most unsettling climatic developments is the warming of the planet and the various weather disturbances it brings in its wake. The list of phenomena routinely cited in the press and on television, which leads us to affirm the reality of global warming, includes:

- The rapid shrinking of frozen surfaces on our planet.[5] The snow layer has diminished by 10% since the end of the 1960s, and at the same time, the period of freezing on lakes and rivers has shortened by two weeks on average. In the northern hemisphere, the duration of sea ice in spring and summer has been reduced by 15%.
- Submarines passing beneath the North Pole have observed a 40% thinning of the pack ice, while mammoth icebergs, as vast as a French county, are breaking loose in the Antarctic and drifting off to melt in the ocean. The facades of glaciers are retreating rapidly up mountainsides. Compare photographs of Chamonix in France at the beginning of the twentieth century with those of today. The melting of ice is a threat to many populated areas, especially in the Himalayas. The eternal snows of Kilimanjaro, so imposing as they look down on herds of elephants in Kenya, are melting away before our eyes, and may not last another twenty years.
- More spectacular still is the frequency of truly violent climatic events: floods, storms, and droughts. The number and cost of natural disasters across the globe has increased enormously. The annual count of floods and cyclones has multiplied five times between 1950 and today. The costs have risen both because of the growing frequency and seriousness of natural disasters and because more and more people tend to live in high-risk zones.

We should also take note of a phenomenon that all nature lovers have come to recognize in their gardens and in the woods: the adaptive response of living things to this rise in temperature. The return of migrating birds, the laying of eggs, and the first appearance of vegetation are occurring noticeably earlier. In the Mediterranean, the buds on leafy trees are opening sixteen days earlier, and the leaves are falling thirteen days later than fifty years ago.[6]

We must still determine the first causes of this warming. It could be argued that warming is due to natural phenomena and not human activity. Indeed, geologists have taught us that the Earth experienced a number of temperature variations in the past: a long succession of glacial periods and warm periods. We might ask the question: could this not be a phase in the millennial cycle?

The concerns about global warming began around 1980, when James Hansen of NASA, on the basis of computer-generated atmospheric models, concluded that the emission of CO_2 and other gases generated from the burning of oil, carbon, and natural gas were raising the world's temperature. This news caused great turmoil in the economic world. It was immediately contested by oil company engineers (especially those from Texas and Saudi Arabia), for whom climatic variations arose entirely from natural causes. Industry, in their opinion, played only a negligible role.

But the alarm had been sounded. The United Nations formed a commission, the Intergovernmental Panel on Climate Change (IPCC), to study the question. More than 2,500 experts from around the globe took part. Their reports were then reviewed by other scientists, and reviewed again at the time of the United Nations' plenary sessions.

In 1995, the IPCC very cautiously presented its preliminary conclusions in the following words: "The weight of evidence suggests a perceptible influence of human activity on the global climate." In February 2008, the IPCC went further: "There is a 90% probability that the warming of the last fifty years is due to human activity."[7]

It would be extremely unwise not to take these conclusions seriously.[8]

Here, the scientific precautionary principle must be respected, especially given that the extent of warming is not easy to evaluate — the reason being that it is difficult to establish accurately the temperatures of the more distant past. However, a number of methods do intersect and indicate that the Earth's average temperature has increased by almost 1°C since the beginning of the twentieth century. The rate of growth has become especially rapid since 1990, and shows no signs of stabilizing.[9]

We have been sorcerers' apprentices. We have set the ball rolling, and it is only now that we are asking ourselves how we can stop it.

Fortunately, science can come to our aid thanks to computer modelling. Many scientific researchers, in particular those of the IPCC, are working on this. Once again, the answers are elusive because of the difficulties inherent in climatology — as we all know from weather reports.[10] The estimates for increases in the Earth's annual average temperature, according to scenarios of human behaviour, go from 1.5 to 5°C and greater for the end of the twenty-first century. According to many climatologists, the situation has already deteriorated to the point where, even if we succeeded in rapidly and effectively limiting the emissions of CO_2, it would take more than a century to halt global warming.

This indicates the seriousness of our situation: global warming could be disastrous for humankind. One might object: the Earth has known other warmings in the past. But what these earlier variations demonstrate is that a difference of only a few degrees is no small matter. On the contrary, during the last ice age, with a decrease of 5°C, the sea level went down by about 120 metres (one could walk from France to England). Canada and northern Europe were covered in glaciers several kilometres thick, like Greenland and the Antarctic today.

THE DANGEROUS INTERPLAY OF CARBON DIOXIDE, WATER VAPOUR, AND METHANE

Global warming could extend far beyond the next century. In the first place, the emission of carbon dioxide could continue until fossil fuels, coal in particular, are depleted. There are still, now, abundant reserves. In the second place, a number of phenomena linked to other gases (called greenhouse gases — we will return to them in Chapter 1), such as water vapour and methane, could exacerbate the warming.

Here is the situation in brief. The increase in temperature hastens the evaporation of ocean water. The water vapour that is released from oceans, rivers, and lakes contributes, in turn, to raising the temperature, which accelerates the evaporation even more, in an ever-increasing cycle.

Even with carbon dioxide emissions and evaporation from oceans and lakes taken into consideration, rapid global warming will be accelerated by the appearance of the sleeping dragon under the polar snows, which would have been better left undisturbed: methane. Permafrost covers vast regions in the high latitudes — Siberia and Canada — where the subsoil is permanently frozen, as summer does not last long enough to melt it. Huge quantities of methane (see Chapter 1, Note 1) are trapped in the crystalline mesh of ice. Methane is a gas that has the capacity to heat up the atmosphere ten times more than CO_2.

Methane already represents more than 5% of the greenhouse effect, and its impact is rapidly growing. Freed by the accelerated melting of the permafrost due to warming, it could have a major influence, and, in concert with CO_2 and water vapour, speed up the process to the point where it reaches very high temperatures.

But we must reiterate that, given our limited knowledge of meteorological matters and our restricted powers of computation, we cannot, today, predict the global temperature that might be produced by these phenomena. Although it is possible that counter-effects could come into play that would reverse the trend,[11] one thing is clear: we are sailing through dangerous waters, and they may very likely become hotter and hotter.

The real problem is the speed with which these processes are taking place. That is the crux of our current dilemma. We will return to this topic often.

THREE SCENARIOS FOR CATASTROPHE

To illustrate our situation, imagine this story: a man is stricken with cancer. Underestimating the seriousness of his condition, he refuses to submit to the usual treatments. To persuade him, the doctor describes to him the catastrophic scenarios that could lie in wait if he does not allow himself to be attended to. He will then make his decision, fully aware of the possible consequences. Of course, nothing is certain. Sometimes cancers develop in unexpected ways and cure themselves spontaneously. Again, we are dealing with the precautionary principle.

We will take the same approach with our patient, the planet Earth, which is suffering from a high fever. The thermometers indicate that its temperature is climbing. Which raises some crucial questions: what temperature will the biosphere reach in the future? What will the effects be? Depending on the maximum temperature attained, we can foresee three different scenarios.

THE DESERT SCENARIO

This scenario applies to a world where, beyond the year 2100, the Earth's average annual temperature has climbed another ten degrees.

Deserts, already expanding rapidly, will increasingly encroach on arable land. We will witness a massive migration of fauna and flora towards the polar regions, where the temperature will remain livable. Only species adapted to desert climates (insects, resistant plants) will continue to survive in lower latitudes. The transition will likely be too rapid for most animals and plants to be able to adapt. Only extreme climate control will permit a few privileged humans to carry on.

In addition, the thermic expansion of water, associated with the melting of ice in Greenland and the Antarctic, could raise the sea level several metres, flooding coastal cities and large low-altitude continental expanses, reducing the amount of habitable land even more (*Figure 0.1*).

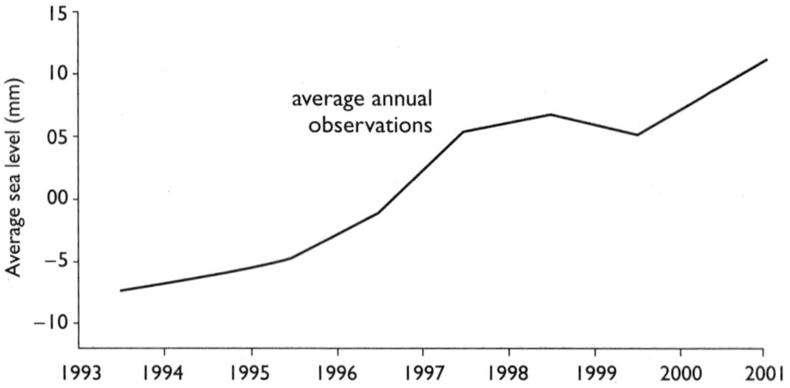

Figure 0.1. The increase in the average sea level between 1993 and 2001 (about 2 centimetres), as measured by the Topex-Poseidon satellite. This increase is due almost entirely to the expansion in the volume of water caused by climatic warming. The melting of continental ice is also a factor, but a very small one.

THE GEYSER SCENARIO

Now imagine that, under the synergistic influence of greenhouse gases, the Earth's average annual temperature were to rise dozens of degrees further. Let us say up to 60 or 70°C. Almost certainly, all multicellular organisms — animals and plants — would perish. Even insects. The proportion of species exterminated would exceed that of all previous extinctions.

There would be one notable exception: bacterial life. Its extraordinary robustness is one of the great discoveries of modern biology. "Extremophiles"[12] is the name we give to those varieties of bacteria that survive under stupefying conditions: the most acidic, alkaline, saline, the most intensely radioactive, and at temperatures approaching the boiling point (100°C) or the freezing point (0°C) of water.

The boiling water intermittently ejected by Icelandic geysers falls back into bluish ponds, where large colonies of blue algae flourish, possibly the first living beings that appeared on our planet. They give us a good picture of primitive life on Earth and its proliferation during the first three billion years of existence. This is the "Geyser Scenario."

Here, we find life on Earth as it may have existed prior to the appearance of the first multicellular organisms (plants and animals). Chronologically, it puts us back about a billion years in biological history. According to this hypothesis, human aggression will have accomplished what no other geological or astronomical activity has been able to do: return life to its bacterial, unicellular beginnings.

Of course, beginning from there, a whole new cosmic adventure could unfold. We can try to imagine it by drawing on our knowledge of the past. The new geological era would be characterized by the biological evolution of primitive cells, more or less analogous to those of a billion years ago. We could conceive that, in conformity with Darwin's schema, they would develop techniques for adaptation over the ages that would be increasingly complex and effective. By analogy with ancient history, unicellular living beings could again join together to form complex organisms, superficially different, no doubt, from those of earlier eras, but still acquiring similar attributes: sensory organs, breathing, digestive and reproductive systems, technical skills. And perhaps, one day, we could exclaim, "Well, well, mankind has come back!" After a long eclipse, we would be there again, and in the course of time we might even behave in such a way as to encounter the same problems we face today. Life on Earth took nearly a billion years to evolve from individual cells to the level of primates, but the sun has almost five billion years left in its cycle before it vaporizes the planets. On a cosmic scale, there would still be time to replay the same scenario.

THE VENUS SCENARIO

The two scenarios already envisaged bring us to a third that would generate an even greater increase in temperature. Here, we must anticipate the worst. We are talking of average annual temperatures well above 100°C. Even the most robust extremophiles would be unable to withstand such extreme temperatures.

We will call this the "Venus Scenario." It is there before us when we admire the magnificent morning or evening star. But its brightness sends us a sombre message, a dramatic warning. Venus is sterile. Observed at close range by space probes, its surface is infernal. The temperature there is 460°C. It rains sulphuric acid.

However inhospitable the environment on Venus, it is Earth's twin to a large degree. The two planets' mass, their distance from the sun, and their quantity of carbon are not that different. But the composition of their atmosphere is radically dissimilar. Venus's atmosphere, composed of carbon dioxide, is responsible for this gigantic greenhouse effect, where no life, such as we know it, is possible.[13]

This is a nightmare scenario, and I would like to offer some reassurance: in the light of our present knowledge, it seems most unlikely. But given what little we know about how the factors involved interact, it would be imprudent to rule it out altogether. Remember that we have chosen, in our exploration, to look at the worst possible case. The Venus Scenario erases four billion years in the growth of cosmic complexity on our planet. We are left with the Earth such as it was in its first hundreds of millions of years, before the deposit of a cover of liquid, before the first molecular reactions that initiated the extraordinary, and still poorly understood, process that gave us the first living cells that dominated the planet for more than three billion years.

Since we are giving our imagination free rein, we can imagine that the process might start up again, and, after billions of years, bring forth life once more. It happened at least once. Why not again? Perhaps plants and animals would reappear. But by this time, the sun would be getting older, time would be limited.

These are three scenarios our sick planet could face if we do not do everything we can to arrest the increase in temperature of the Earth's atmosphere. All that, I repeat, is within the realm of the possible.

We have just exercised our powers of imagination. It's a precious faculty with which we have been endowed. It's possible that we might use it to avoid succumbing to a runaway greenhouse effect. I hope we will, and in fact, I believe we can, even if it's very hard to say how. We must use all our resources to stop this warming. We must act quickly if we want to give humanity its best chance to continue its extraordinary adventure on Earth.

This means painful choices and drastic measures. We must ask ourselves: are we prepared to forego the many advantages and comforts of modern life? What political party will be courageous enough to build into its program a massive reduction of automobile traffic or energy production? Can we imagine a reversal of our thrust towards ever more energy production? Can we, for our own good, call the retreat?

As history has shown, man always waits to be confronted with a catastrophe before drastically changing his attitude.

> *"To protect the environment costs a lot.*
> *To do nothing will cost much more."*
> Kofi Annan

PUTTING THE BRAKES ON TEMPERATURE

We are facing a crucial question: what could stop a warming process that has already gathered considerable momentum thanks to human activity? There are two possibilities: one pessimistic, the other optimistic.

We'll let the pessimist go first. Since the warming is primarily due to human activity, we may suppose that the disappearance of this species — or its considerable diminishment[14] — would stop the warming (although we cannot rule out the possibility of a snowballing that could continue for a long time). This simply means that we will have paid the price for the crisis and will be absent during the era to follow, like the dinosaurs after the fall of the meteorite in Mexico, sixty-five million years ago. The difference, however, is that they were responsible for nothing.

Nature, it is said, is unforgiving. No species is immune to extinction. Millions of species have been born, have thrived, and have disappeared from the planet since the beginning of life on Earth. Life goes on without them. It is a normal part of biological evolution on our planet.

The criterion for permanence is simple: those species that have established a harmonious relationship with their environment, with the ecosystem of which they are a part, survive. What is needed is a fair exchange: giving and receiving.

My favourite example is the tortoise. It has existed for three hundred million years, and is threatened by no one, other than humans.

Where harmony with the biosphere is concerned, as a species, we trail far behind. One might say with reason that the Earth is infested with human beings (much more lethal than sharks).

A healthy planet encounters a sick planet:
"What happened to you?"
"Don't ask! I've caught a bad illness called 'humanity!'"
"Don't worry, I've had it before. It cures itself. It'll go away."

To raise our spirits, I will now outline the optimistic solution. It's what we hope for with all our hearts, and it's what so many people are working towards today. It represents a global return to sanity, to a humankind that is at last responsible and resolved to put an end to the deterioration of its habitat, and in such a way that it does not eliminate itself.

Throughout this book, after having described as objectively as possible the state of the planet, we will try to indicate the progress that has already been made, and the various practical measures that could help us to achieve our goal.

The task will be long, arduous, costly, and full of pitfalls. Initiatives that appear worthwhile could fail to deliver the results we hoped for. We must navigate by eye, testing the wind, careful about what we do. Once again, we are heading into a very dangerous zone.

We can be encouraged by the fact that concrete results have already been obtained when scientists, business people, and governments have agreed to recognize a problem and have undertaken to resolve it on an international scale. Two examples: the hole in the ozone layer, and acid rain. Not that these problems have been solved completely (we will have more to say about them further on), but progress has been made. This tripartite agreement (scientists, industry, governments) is the precondition for planetary recuperation — without it, nothing will change. The goal of all environmental movements must be to broker such agreements as rapidly as possible.

We cannot ignore the fact that there are many who dispute the gravity of our situation.

Let us first recognize that different opinions must be aired in any scientific debate, especially if there are economic implications and costly initiatives proposed. It is also important to assess as objectively as possible the arguments being put forth.

The most important and the most active dissenting group was the Global Climate Coalition, which, over a period of ten years, brought together oil companies, and coal and energy producers from around the globe in an effort to minimize the gravity of the situation and to pin the blame on natural phenomena. However, after the reports of the IPCC, companies such as Shell, Amoco, and British Petroleum withdrew from the coalition, which has since collapsed.[15] Subsequently, companies such as DuPont, British Petroleum, Amoco, and Shell have invested in renewable energy, while Toyota in Japan has tried to go beyond the goals of the Kyoto Accord in reducing gas emissions.

Some people continue, as is their right, to deny the risks to the planet. In a book that received a great deal of media attention, Danish scientist, Bjørn Lomborg, (see Chapter 6, Note 7) asserts that, contrary to the alarmist discourse of the ecologists, humanity continues to make progress.

The progress Lomborg refers to is real. Economies are prospering all over the world. Democracy and social progress are increasingly gaining ground. The production of grains has increased considerably over the last half-century. The average lifespan is climbing. Urban atmospheric pollution is diminishing.

There are, however, some serious qualifications to be made. As we will see in Chapter 3, the production of food in the world has been stagnant or in decline for the last ten years, while, according to the predictions of demographers, the global population will not level off before the middle of the twenty-first century.

Many of the advances cited by Lomborg only affect rich countries. The average lifespan in the former Soviet Union is, in fact, falling, as it is in sub-Saharan Africa (see Chapter 6). Pollution in cities is being reduced in rich countries, but is growing rapidly in poor countries. Just take a walk in Delhi or Bangkok, and you will regret not wearing a gas mask. Have we the right, from the high ground of our own comfortable existence, to ignore four-fifths of the human population?

But the most important point is that most of these economic, social, and political advances have been made at the cost of a rapid deterioration of the environment, which may no longer be able to support them. Given the fact that global reserves are not limitless, the expression "lasting economic growth" is an absurdity. The improvement in the quality of life in poor countries is, in itself, excellent news. But the facts are clear. If the Chinese and Indians had as many cars per family as Americans and Europeans, the consumption of fuel and the emission of carbon dioxide would reach catastrophic proportions. Add to that the enormous disparity in the living conditions of different populations. Fewer than 15% of humans consume 80% of our natural resources. The number of human beings who live below the poverty line increases every year. We will have more to say about the threat this disparity poses to the biosphere's future. It may represent the greatest danger of all.

A book like Lomborg's, in my opinion, plays a very harmful role by encouraging inaction at a very crucial juncture, when large-scale mobilization is an absolute necessity.

Once again, it's not a question of playing the prophet of doom, but of alerting the public, and political leaders to the catastrophic risks we are running, as we continue to behave as though nothing serious were hanging over our heads. We must not harbour the illusion inherited from scientism that we will inevitably, in the future, find solutions to all the problems that we cause. When animal and plant species disappear, it is already too late. If we are one day faced with an uncontrollable acceleration of the greenhouse effect, it will also be too late to save the human species.

1

CHANGE OF AIR, CHANGE OF ERA

ONE OF THE GREAT DANGERS of the current crisis is rooted in the notorious greenhouse effect, widely blamed for overheating our planet.

However, this same phenomenon made life on Earth possible. It is still indispensable. But our gas emissions are pushing it too far. The poison is in the dose.

To hasten the sprouting of seeds in spring, a gardener puts them in a greenhouse, covering them with a pane of glass. The yellow light of the sun passes through the glass and is absorbed and transformed into heat by the soil, raising its temperature. The soil gives off heat through infrared rays that the glass will not let escape. It is transparent to yellow photons, but opaque to infrared photons. That is what creates the greenhouse effect.

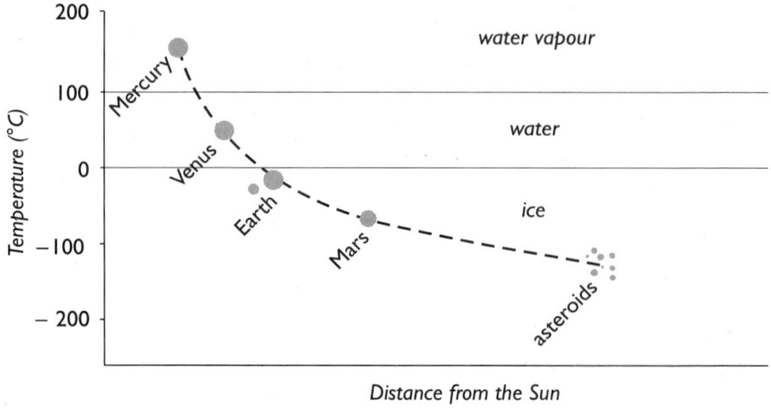

Figure 1.1. An outline of the temperatures on the surface of planets in our solar system. This figure shows the progressive drop in average temperature due to distancing from the sun, with no atmosphere factored in. The "livable" zone is the region where the temperature ranges from 0 to 100°C, where water can exist in a liquid state. Below that, it is ice; above, it is water vapour. We see that without their atmospheres, the Earth would be iced over (at -15°C), while Venus would be within the livable zone.

The same thing happens to the Earth. Carbon dioxide, water vapour, methane, and several other greenhouse gases[1] form a layer that replicates the effect of the pane of glass. The result: the temperature rises on the Earth's surface. It is interesting to note that the appearance of life on Earth is closely tied to this phenomenon. Without the presence of greenhouse gases in our atmosphere, the average temperature on the Earth's surface would be -15°C. But that's not all: when the Earth was born, the sun was colder than it is today; its colour was closer to orange than to today's yellow. As a result, the quantity of solar energy received by the Earth was smaller (75% of today's figure). Without the greenhouse effect caused by the presence of gas, water would have stayed frozen, like on Jupiter's satellites (*Figures 1.1 and 1.2*).

Our neighbours, Mars and Venus, have atmospheres largely made up of carbon dioxide. It is generally agreed that this must have been the case in our primitive atmosphere as well. The same gas was likely

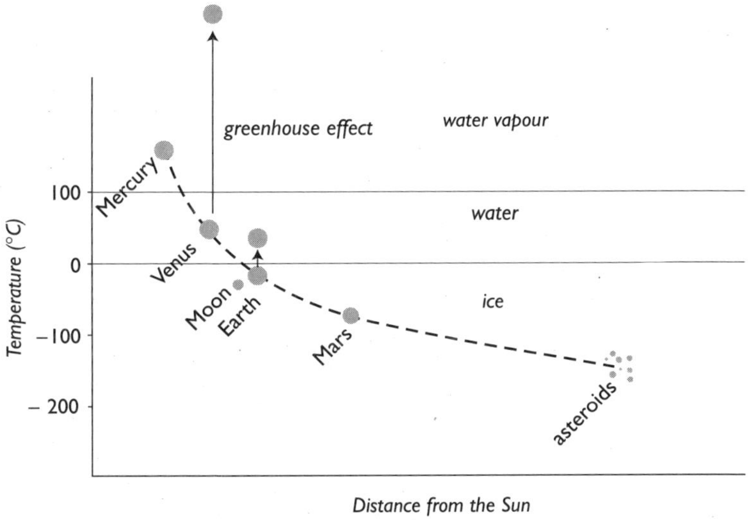

Figure 1.2. This is the same schema as Figure 1.1, but here we take into account the presence of atmospheres and the greenhouse effect that they generate. This time, the Earth finds itself in the livable zone, while the moon (with no atmosphere) remains in the icy zone. On the other hand, its atmosphere of carbon dioxide places the planet Venus in the vapour zone: its surface is 460°C. Mars may once have existed in the livable zone. Today its atmosphere is too thin for it to be found there.

responsible for our early greenhouse effect. It is also possible that methane played a role.

ICE AGES AND TEMPERATE PERIODS

In its beginning, the Earth was doubtlessly a ball of molten lava. But it seems that it cooled rapidly, and that liquid water appeared some two hundred million years after its birth, which took place 4.5 billion years ago.[2] The oldest traces of life appeared hundreds of millions of years later, between 3.8 and 3.5 billion years ago.[3]

The first living beings, microscopic aquatic organisms, used the light of the sun to combine carbon dioxide with water to produce organic matter. Oxygen was given off, and it gradually enriched the atmosphere.

This component became significant about two billion years ago.[4]

The oldest determinations of temperature take us back three billion years (*Figure 1.3*). The first ice ages occurred about two billion years ago.

Periods of warming and glaciation have alternated ever since. The closer we get to the present day, the more abundant and accurate the data is.

Our most accurate observations go back several million years. These are based on the study of ocean sediment. We learn that between one billion (the appearance of the first organisms) and ten million years ago (the appearance of the prehominoids), the Earth's average annual

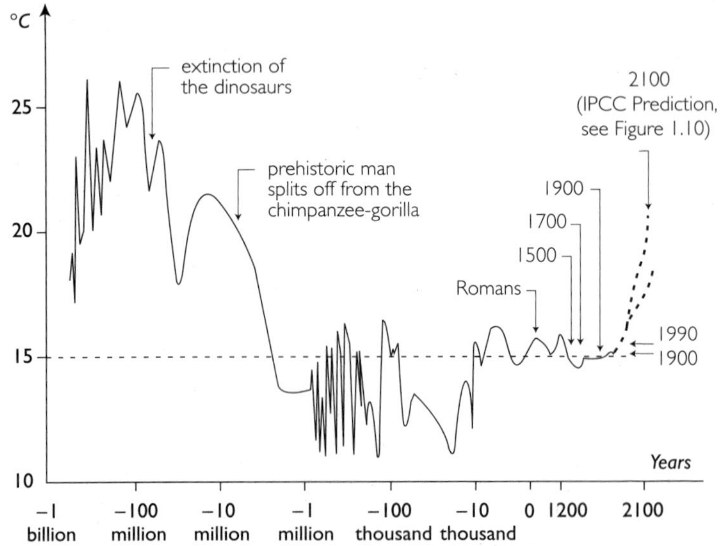

Figure 1.3. The evolution of the average temperature on the surface of the Earth for the last hundreds of millions of years (note that the time scale is compressed). The period from 500 million to 5 million years ago is from 5 to 10° hotter than now. To the right (the last million years), we see the sequence of glacial and temperate periods, which continue to the present day.

Source: Fritz Gassmann, *Effet de serre*, Zurich, Georg Éditeur, 1994.

temperature often exceeded 20°C, and sometimes 25°C. That is 5 to 10°C higher than its current value.

Ice cores from the Antarctic give us more exact data concerning the later period. Each level of the core corresponds to a well-defined period, and analyses reveal temperature change and the presence of methane and carbon dioxide (*Figures 1.4 and 1.5*). We observe that the glacial periods appear, on average, every hundred thousand years, separated by warmer periods of about twenty thousand years. But in each of these periods, we note a superimposition of much more rapid variations that give the impression of chaotic behaviour.

For the last million years, the average temperature has barely risen above its current value (14°C).

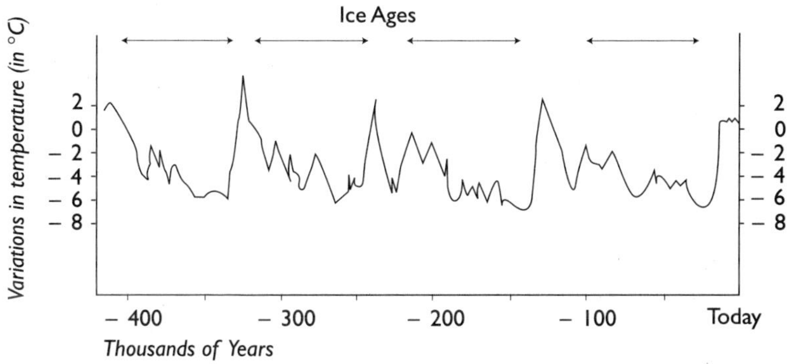

Figure 1.4. Evolution of the average temperature on Earth for the last 400,000 years. Notice the recurring appearance of ice ages about every 100,000 years. This phenomenon is generally attributed to the slow variation in sunshine due to cyclical variations in the properties of the Earth's orbit around the sun (ellipticity, obliquity).

This alternation between hot and cold is likely linked to variations in the Earth's orbit around the sun. On a scale of some tens of thousands of years, the Earth's orbit becomes more or less elliptical, and changes its orientation with regard to the sun. The result is a variation in the

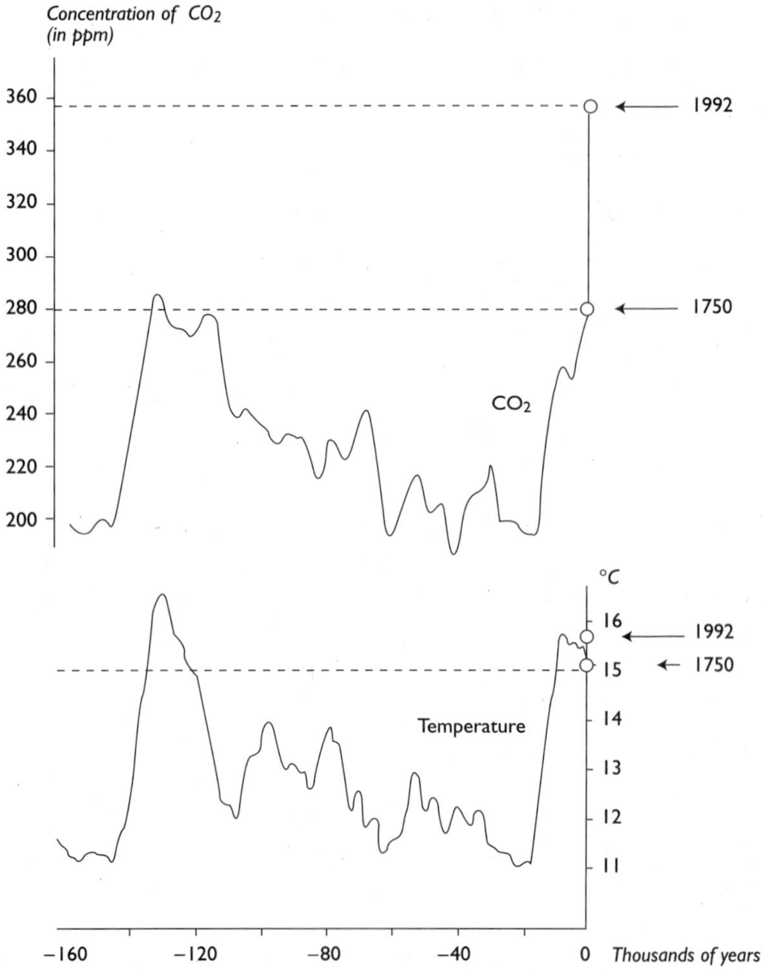

Figure 1.5. Temperature and carbon dioxide measured in the glacial cores of the Antarctic, corresponding to the last 160,000 years. Note the correlation between the two readings.

average sunlight reaching the Earth, and, therefore, in the temperature of the Earth's surface. This correlation between the Earth's orbit and the ice ages was proposed for the first time by Milutin Milanković, and today is generally accepted.[5]

The Antarctic cores have provided us with precious information: an excellent correlation between temperature and the concentration of greenhouse gases (carbon dioxide and methane) clearly demonstrates the relationship between these factors.

The last ice age ended about ten thousand years ago. The ice covered the north of Europe as far south as England, as well as much of North America. It was during the last days of this glacial period that the artists of Lascaux and Vallon-Pont-d'Arc executed their magnificent rock paintings. The entrance to the Cosquer grotto is 46 metres below today's sea level, which clearly indicates that the sea level was much lower at that time than now. The ice field monopolized a significant proportion of the oceanic mass.

We are living today in a warm phase of our climate's history. A cooling trend should soon begin.[6] But this natural cooling generally takes place at a rate of about 1°C per thousand years, while current warming is much more rapid.[7] The temperature has risen close to 1°C in a half-century (from 13.84°C in 1950 to 14.6°C in 2004). And the process

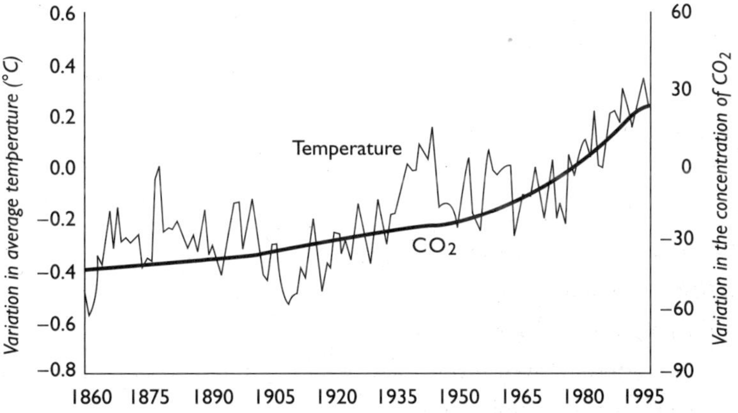

Figure 1.6. Variation in average temperature on the surface of the Earth between 1860 and 2000.

SOURCE: GODDARD INSTITUTE FOR SPACE STUDIES, NASA.

is speeding up. The warmest ten years took place between 1998 and 2007 (*Figure 1.6*).

It would appear that the shifting of the Earth's orbit will not be of much help in delaying the warming caused by human activity.

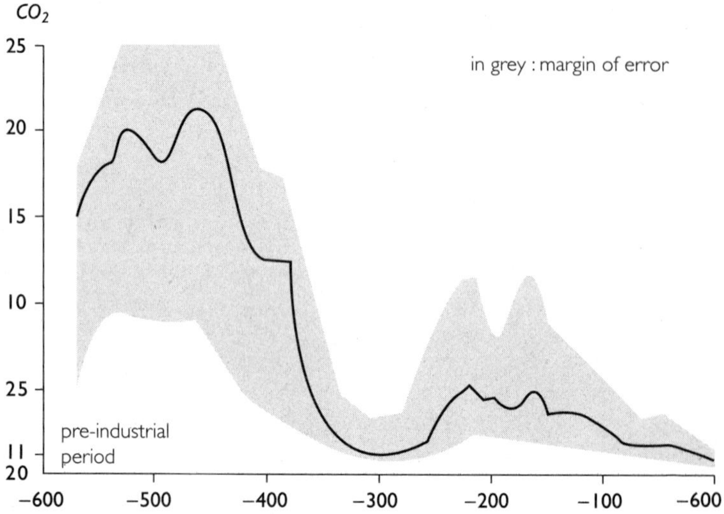

Figure 1.7. Evolution in the concentration of carbon dioxide (CO_2) on the Earth's surface through the geologic ages, by comparison with the pre-industrial figure (1 on the scale at the left). Between 600 and 300 million years ago, the concentration of carbon dioxide was ten to twenty times higher than its current value.

SOURCE: AEN, INFO, 2000.

Some experts advocate natural causes for the warming, associated largely with solar activity. Many studies have investigated a possible contribution of certain solar effects to climate change, including variations in cosmic radiation and in the solar magnetic field (which has doubled over the last century). Solar phenomena may have played a role in certain climatic episodes in the past. But the most qualified experts agree that the contribution of these natural factors to the current greenhouse effect is minimal[8] when compared to that of human industry.

The increase in man-made carbon dioxide emissions is the principal cause of this warming. Before the industrial age, there was a relative balance between the quantities of CO_2 absorbed and expelled by the sea and the earth, which allowed the atmosphere to maintain a proportion of CO_2 that was more or less constant. This component varied over the geologic ages (*Figure 1.7*). During the warm periods between six hundred and four hundred million years ago (the primary and secondary eras), the CO_2 level was about ten times higher than it is today on average. As we saw earlier, this ratio correlated well with the temperature during the last great ice ages. Since the beginning of the twentieth century, the proportion of carbon dioxide has increased by more than 25%. It is increasing still: the years 2006 and 2007 broke all previous records. Today, the level is higher than it has been for 400,000 years (*Figure 1.8*).

Since we know that CO_2 levels have already been fifteen times higher than today, why can we not assume that the ocean will absorb our

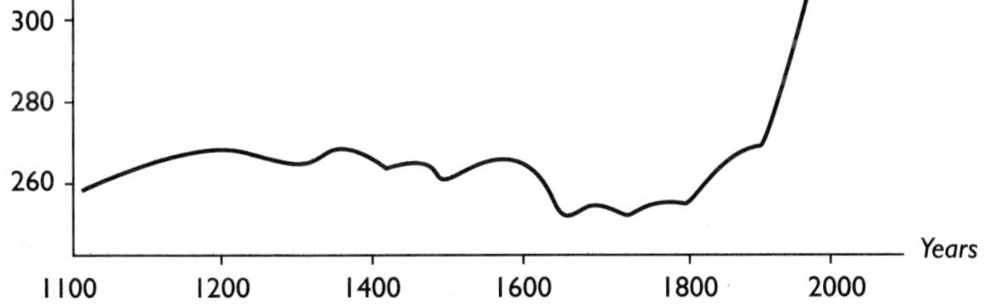

Figure 1.8. The concentration of carbon dioxide in the atmosphere since the year 1100. Its rapid rise began with the industrial age. Today, the concentration is the highest it has been for the last 400,000 years. It could go on to double over the next century if nothing is done to control it.

emissions of industrial gas? It's a question of speed. It takes a very long time to re-establish an equilibrium. Even if we were to stop the emissions of CO_2, it would take several hundred years to regain this balance. That's the whole problem. Today, the earth and the sea absorb only half the emissions.[9] To arrest the increase in CO_2 in the atmosphere, we would have to reduce the emissions by half and go back to the level of 1935. Only on this condition could we stabilize the temperature. The goal of the Kyoto agreement, which was much more modest, was to reduce emissions by 6%, to the level of 1990 (*Figure 1.9*). After much waffling, the agreement was ratified in 2005, despite the United States, but thanks to Russia, the second greatest emitter in the world (17%).

THE SEQUESTRATION OF CARBON DIOXIDE

One way to control the growing amount of CO_2 that is accumulating in the atmosphere would be to sequester it.

The most natural method of sequestering CO_2 is, of course, to plant new forests: the plants would extract carbon dioxide from the air and trap it in their tissues. The problem is that this sequestration is short-term. When the plant dies, the CO_2 is released into the atmosphere. This solution only delays the problem. According to recent studies, this delay would in fact be very brief, a few years on average.[10]

A more daring solution is to channel the carbon dioxide produced by thermal power stations directly into the ocean, bypassing the atmosphere. Several groups are working on this. Others propose putting nitrates into the sea to fertilize the marine plankton so they will absorb more CO_2. This project has been largely discredited. Its impact would be small, while the effects on the ocean's fauna and flora could be great; even catastrophic. It's the sorcerer's apprentice all over again.[11]

Year	Emissions	CO_2
1950	1,612	n/a
1955	2,013	n/a
1960	2,535	316.7
1965	3,087	319.9
1970	3,997	325.5
1971	4,143	326.2
1972	4,031	327.3
1973	4,538	329.5
1974	4,545	330.1
1975	4,518	331.0
1976	4,776	332.0
1977	4,910	333.7
1978	4,950	335.3
1979	5,229	336.7
1980	5,155	338.5
1981	4,984	339.8
1982	4,947	341.0
1983	4,933	342.6
1984	5,098	344.2
1985	5,271	345.7
1986	5,453	347.0
1987	5,574	348.7
1988	5,789	351.3
1989	5,892	352.7
1990	5,931	354.0
1991	6,020	355.5
1992	5,879	356.4
1993	5,861	357.0
1994	6,013	358.9
1995	6,190	360.9
1996	6,315	362.6
1997	6,395	363.8
1998	6,381	366.6
1999	6,340	368.3
2000	6,299	369.4

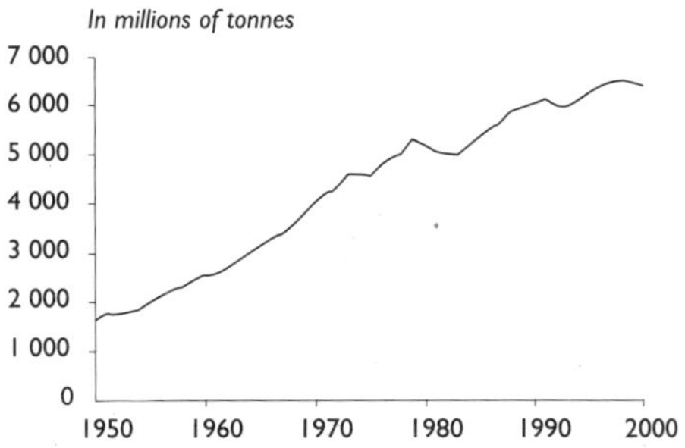

Emissions of CO_2

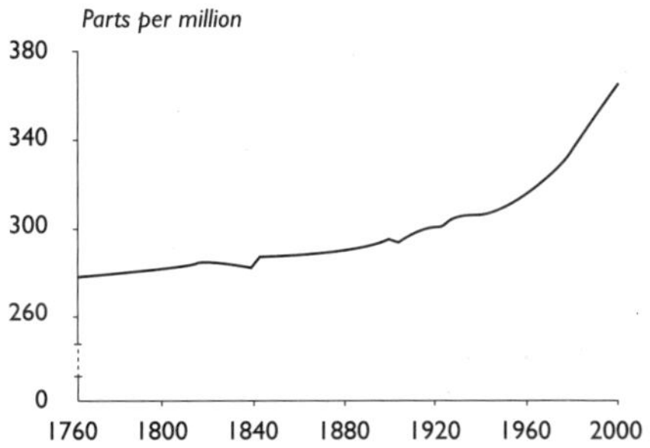

Concentration of CO_2

Figure 1.9. Annual emissions of carbon dioxide (in millions of tonnes of carbon) since 1950, and the concentration of this gas in the atmosphere (parts per million).

THE SHORT-TERM EFFECTS OF GLOBAL WARMING

In the prologue, I listed the visible effects of global warming, as well as its disastrous consequences, both medium- and long-term. We now have scientific models that study the possible short-term effects of warming, on the scale, for instance, of one human generation. The first test of these models' reliability is their capacity to correctly reproduce the meteorological conditions of the past. That is what they are doing up to a certain point, since they have succeeded in reconstituting the average temperatures of the Earth's surface going back more than a hundred years. But we must re-emphasize that uncertainties still remain, which, however, should lessen over time.[12]

Scientific studies seem to agree that small changes in the average temperature on the surface of the globe — even 1 or 2°C — would alter the climate and meteorological conditions (*Figure 1.10*). The rise in temperatures would be disastrous for agriculture in tropical or semi-tropical regions, where food is already scarce (see *The Desert Scenario*, page 9). The Arctic would be an open summer ocean in 2050, which would have one happy consequence, a Northwest Passage that would shorten the sea journey between New York and Tokyo by 5,000 kilometres.

A number of models predict heat waves, floods, droughts or violent storms, an elevation of the sea level, and more extreme meteorological cycles such as the El Niño phenomenon, already so disastrous in 1997.[13] The unusual frequency and violence of the cyclones in the West Indies and Japan in the autumn of 2004 is mostly likely one of the consequences, as is the case of Hurricane Katrina, which destroyed much of New Orleans in 2005.

Beyond deadly meteorological phenomena, there is also a concern for human health. These disturbances encourage the development of certain illnesses, such as malaria and cholera.[14] East Africa, normally a dry zone, is a good example. In 1997, as a result of El Niño, unusual rainfalls drowned the herds and brought cholera to the capital of Kenya.

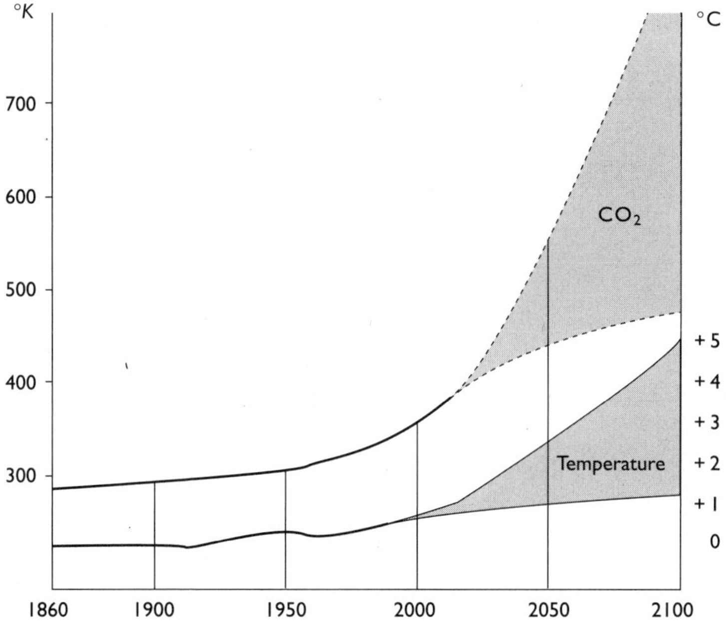

Figure 1.10. Estimate of the increase in temperature and carbon dioxide to the year 2100, taking uncertainties into consideration. The upper curve represents the situation if the increase in carbon dioxide is not controlled. The lower curve represents the minimum values that might be expected if the emissions are greatly reduced.

SOURCE: TIME MAGAZINE, NOVEMBER 1997.

What is more, past examples teach us that the climatic system can generate surprising events, including the slowing, or even the stoppage, of certain major ocean currents such as the Gulf Stream,[15] which today carries tropical heat towards northern regions, or a sudden change in temperature on the scale of a hemisphere, at least, over a single human generation.

Let's return for a moment to the dragon buried in the ice, methane. We know for a fact that enormous quantities are sequestered not only in the permafrost, but also in undersea deposits near the continents — the continental shelves. Some see these as a possible source of fossil fuels. But the freeing of this gas through the melting of ice and the destabilization of these undersea depths — very likely if the temperature continues to climb — could trigger a rapid warming of the atmosphere. The short lifespan of this gas in the atmosphere (it is destroyed within ten years by molecular reaction with other gases) could, in part, neutralize this effect if methane is not released too quickly. But whatever happens, it will end up as CO_2 and add to the atmospheric mass of that gas.[16]

THE HOLE IN THE OZONE LAYER

Another serious ecological problem associated with the atmosphere, one we have not yet talked about, is the famous hole in the ozone layer.

Ozone is a type of oxygen made up of three atoms, unlike the one we breathe, which contains two. It is present in our atmosphere at two different altitudes (*Figure 1.11*).

There is, first of all, the ozone layer hovering between twenty and fifty kilometres over our heads. It is called high-altitude ozone, or "good ozone." It intercepts the sun's ultraviolet radiation, which would make life on Earth impossible. This layer did not exist in our planet's infancy.[17] It appeared at the same time as atmospheric oxygen, about two billion years ago. Its protective cloak enabled aquatic animals to come out of the water and populate the continents.

A second layer of ozone may be found at low altitude in the atmosphere, on the planet's surface. It is called "bad ozone."

First, the good ozone, and the problems posed by holes in the protective shield that preserves human life. The thickness of the ozone layer at high altitude has been measured routinely for decades over the South Pole by the British Antarctic Survey. Beginning in 1985, a recurring thinning was observed every spring (*Figure 1.12*). The alert was given, and NASA satellites orbiting over the layer made similar observations,

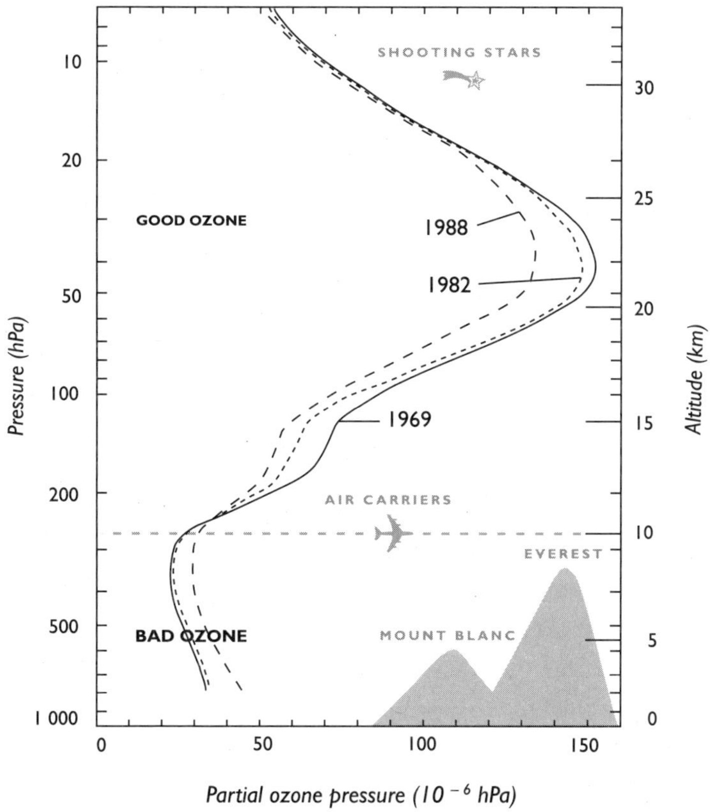

Figure 1.11. The density of atmospheric ozone in terms of altitude. We observe the layer of "good ozone," several dozen kilometres high, as well as the layer of "bad ozone" on the Earth's surface. The three curves, more or less parallel, show the variations in concentration in 1969, 1982, and 1988. The good ozone has diminished, while the bad ozone has increased. To complete the picture, we indicate the elevation of the highest mountains, that of commercial airliners, and of shooting stars.

confirmed the results, and demonstrated that the situation was continuing to deteriorate. The spring shrinkage continues to this day, sometimes exceeding 70%. The phenomenon occurs elsewhere over the plane, but on a lesser scale.[18]

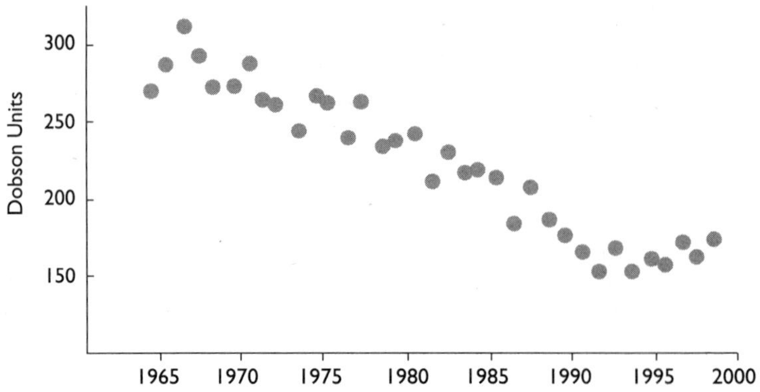

Figure 1.12. The average level of "good" ozone over the Antarctic since 1965. Note the drop from 1980–1990. Today (2008), this thickness seems to have slowly stabilized.

Because it permits increasingly large quantities of ultraviolet rays to reach the ground, the shrinking of the ozone layer can have very harmful effects: an increase in skin cancers and a deterioration in plant life crucial for the food chain.

We have excellent reasons to believe that this progressive destruction is due to human activity. Gases produced by industry, in particular CFCs,[19] are responsible. Accumulating in the atmosphere, they climb to the stratosphere, where they are destroyed by solar ultraviolet radiation, producing chlorine molecules, rapid destroyers of ozone.

These gases, once used in aerosols and refrigerators, are now banned. During the 1970s, they were being manufactured to the tune of nearly a million tonnes per year. This production multiplied the presence of chlorine in the atmosphere by six between 1950 and 1990. The alarm was then raised by the scientific community, and in 1987, 150 countries ratified the Montreal Protocol that banned the production of CFCs and encouraged research that would provide a replacement (*Figure 1.13*).

Here we should call attention to an important fact that we must keep in mind as we proceed: we were able to do something. When scientists, governments, and industry pool their resources to resolve a problem, significant progress can be made. We will see this elsewhere. We must emphasize this so as not to despair. We must demonstrate that all is not lost if we get down to work in time with a single-mindedness and an energy appropriate to the gravity of the situation.

The effects of the Montreal moratorium remain uncertain. Measurements made by NASA between 1979 and 2003 show a reduction in the concentration of gases harmful to the ozone. The rate of ozone destruction also seems to be slowing. According to measurements made by ESA's Envisat satellite in 2007, the hole appears to have shrunk by 20% with respect to the previous year. But we must be patient. It could take more than a century for it to recover lost ground.

The ban on CFCs is being half-heartedly respected by most Eastern and developing countries. Significant traffic in CFCs has developed over the last ten years, especially via the East. Unfortunately, for some, short-term economic advantage has remained the top priority, to the detriment of the ecological balance required by the planet.

What is more, a recent study has revealed that concentrations of greenhouse gases generated by human activity — primarily CO_2 — play a role in reducing stratospheric ozone. The climatic change resulting from greenhouse gas emissions also has harmful consequences for the

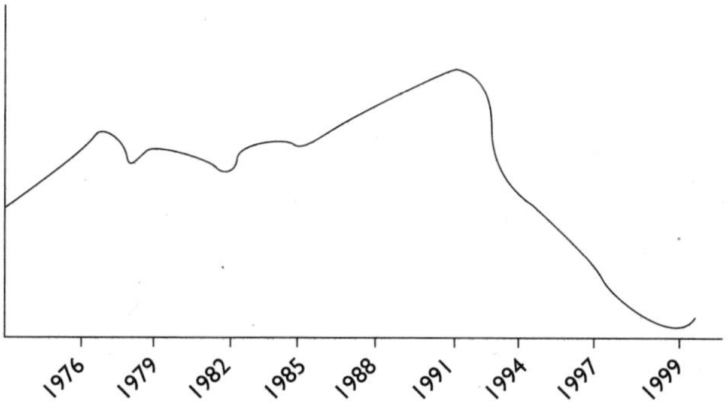

Figure 1.13. World production of CFCs since 1976.

ozone layer. There's a reason for this. If greenhouse gases increase the surface temperature, they also cool the higher layers of the atmosphere. Cold temperatures precipitate the destruction of stratospheric ozone. Climatic change could therefore slow the complete repair of the ozone layer, which we anticipate in the second half of the twenty-first century.[20]

All of which says this about nature's ecological balance: you only need to affect one part of it for the entire picture to be disturbed.

BAD OZONE

Let us now move on to low-altitude ozone, or bad ozone. What we call bad ozone is produced naturally by storms, and by the nitrogen oxides and hydrocarbons emitted by automobiles. Road traffic has generated considerable quantities, but, curiously, they are often more significant in rural regions near cities than in the cities themselves (*Figure 1.14*).

We call it bad ozone because of its harmful effects on living things. Through its oxidizing power, it modifies the permeability of cellular membranes and disturbs photosynthesis and breathing. In this way, it affects the life of trees (the yellow discoloration of pine needles in Mediterranean forests). In humans, it causes irritation of the eyes, mucous membranes, and the respiratory system.

It must be recognized that in most European countries, anti-pollution standards imposed on motor vehicles have helped significantly reduce this ozone pollution. But that is not the case in many megacities of the developing world. In Mexico City, for example, the ozone standards are exceeded 337 days per year. There, security measures have been compromised by the black market and by the corruption of falsified vehicle inspections.

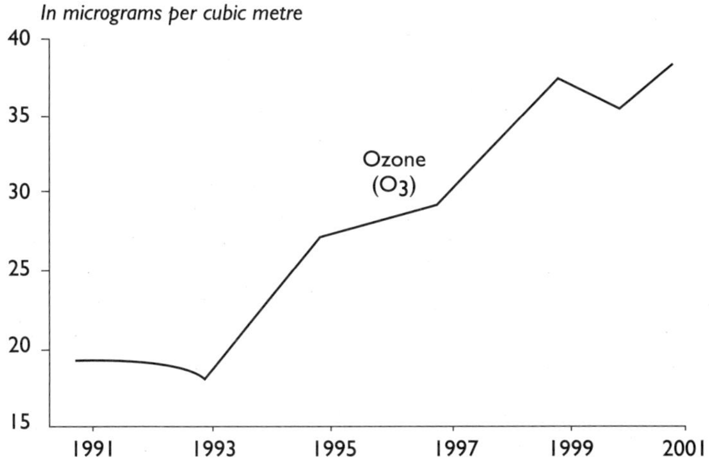

Figure 1.14. A record of bad ozone concentration in Parisian air since 1991. This ozone is largely due to road traffic.

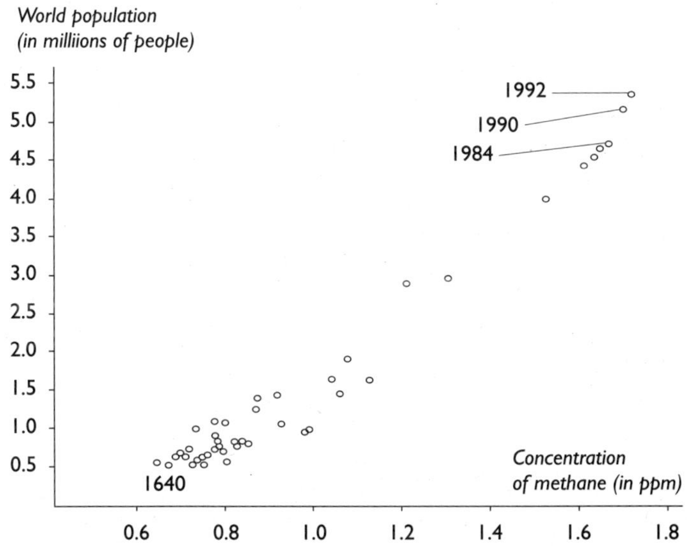

Figure 1.15. A record of methane concentration in the Earth's atmosphere since 1640, correlated with human population.

OTHER ATMOSPHERIC POLLUTION

In addition to CO_2, methane (*Figure 1.15*), and CFCs, many harmful substances are introduced into the atmosphere by human activity. There is sulphur dioxide, nitrogen oxides, mercury, solid particles, persistent organic pollutants, and volatile organic compounds. The use of fossil fuels (in power stations and the transport sector), the incineration of urban and medical waste, and the smelting of sulphurated metal-bearing ore are responsible for large quantities of atmospheric pollutants.

After a major crisis in the 1950s and 1960s (in December of 1952, smog caused more than four thousand deaths in London) great progress was made in Europe and North America (*Figure 1.16*). But such was not the case in the developing world. I was recently in Datong, in the north of China. The sky was a constant dirty yellow. I don't know if children there even know that the colour of the sky is supposed to be blue. Eight of the ten most polluted cities in the world are in China. Elsewhere, the situation is also dire. Breathing in New Delhi is equivalent to smoking ten to twenty cigarettes a day.

The terrible discomfort this pollution generates locally does not stop at the borders of a district or a state. Many pollutants that threaten

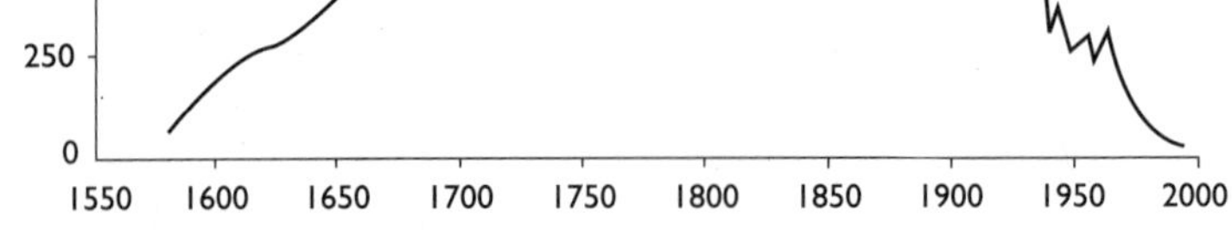

Figure 1.16. Sulphur dioxide (SO_2) in London since 1550. Generated by urban heating, this gas caused the death of more than four thousand people in 1952. A law on air pollution has since improved the situation considerably.

human health and the well-being of ecosystems are transported dozens, or even thousands, of kilometres by air currents. A pollution cloud twenty times larger than France was recently discovered by satellite over the Indian Ocean. It was produced by atmospheric emissions from India and China.[21]

ACID RAIN: A PROBLEM BEING SOLVED

The problem of acid rain originated with coal-fuelled power stations. The oxides of nitrogen and sulphur — sulphur dioxide in particular — and the acid aerosols emitted by their chimneys mixed with water vapour to form acidic precipitation. These rains damaged forests and plants by acidifying bodies of water, and they attacked stone and cement structures.

In the beginning, to avoid local pollution, very high chimneys were constructed. A dubious solution. Picked up by high-altitude winds, the emissions travelled thousands of kilometres. The result? The destruction of great forests and the death of fish in bodies of water. This phenomenon became particularly serious in North America around 1980. In Quebec, I saw lake waters in the far north turn from green to the blue of southern seas. This shift in colour signalled the disappearance of a large proportion of soft-water plankton.

Following vigorous protests, the problem was finally taken seriously. The solution arrived around 1990 (*Figure 1.17*). It became mandatory to place filters on the tops of high chimneys. Today, the situation has largely been remedied in North America (*Figure 1.18*) and in Western Europe. In France, for example, sulphur oxides are in decline. But this is not so in Eastern Europe, in the ex-Soviet Union, and, above all, in China. The Japanese are looking on in despair as acid rain generated by Chinese power stations and blown across the Sea of Japan destroys their beautiful sacred forests.

Along with the anticipated repair of the ozone layer, this is another example of, at least partial, success, showing that solutions are possible on the condition, once more, that there is widespread agreement among the parties concerned: political, scientific, and industrial. But, as is so often the case, these improvements are restricted to rich countries. Poor developing nations get few of the benefits.

But even in Western countries, despite the improvements we have seen, acid rain remains a problem due to the continuing growth of road transport, domestic vehicles, and trucking. The political decision to favour this mode of transportation risks neutralizing the progress made. It is, as of now, the main cause of nitric acid emissions and the formation of atmospheric ozone. Forests and lakes are still in danger.

Another improvement worth mentioning concerns lead, which, along with the exhaust from our cars, has become a significant component of the air we breathe. Since the introduction of unleaded gas, in some countries at least, its concentration has been cut to a third of what it was.

The list of pollutants in the air is unfortunately very long. But what is most unsettling by far, today, is the global warming that disturbs the climate and ecosystems, and that can cause irreversible damage.

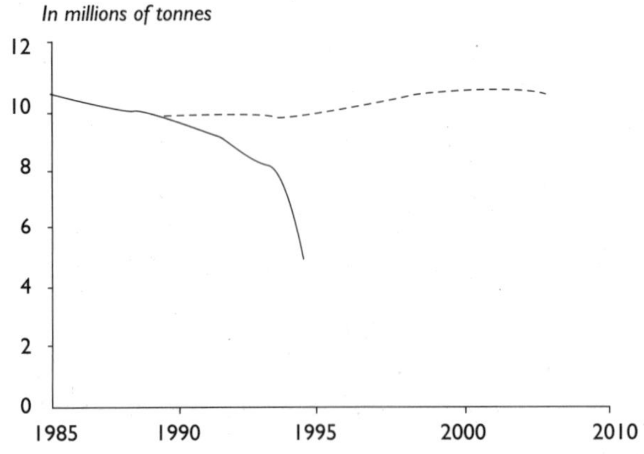

Figure 1.17. The decrease in sulphur dioxide (SO_2) in the United States after the 1990 legislation on emissions from power generator smokestacks. The dotted curve shows the probable trend had there been no legislation. Sulphur dioxide generates acid rain.

ORIGINS AND HISTORY OF THE ATMOSPHERE

We do not see the air, but we feel it when the wind blows. For millennia, it remained a mystery. About 2,500 years ago, Aristotle described it as a "subtle substance" that filled the universe to the celestial vault.

It was not until the seventeenth century that, thanks to the development of appropriate tools for measurement, we began to learn its properties. In 1640, Evangelista Torricelli discovered that, despite its subtlety and apparent lightness, atmosphere had weight. Blaise Pascal showed that this weight diminished progressively as one moved to a higher altitude. Conclusion: air does not fill the universe. It forms a thin layer one 100 kilometres thick on the surface of the Earth, the radius of which is 8,000 kilometres. The setting sun illuminates the thin film of gas that surrounds our planet. This film is our habitat in the universe. It is what we must care for if we want to survive in this world.

What is the nature of the gas that makes up our atmosphere? The birth of chemistry at the end of the eighteenth century enabled us to do the analysis. There, we find mainly nitrogen (about 80%), and oxygen (about 20%). But also, in very small quantities, carbon dioxide, water vapour, and methane. Despite their rarity, these gases are important factors in the future of our planet.

Thanks to the progress in planetology, we can try to retrace the origins of the atmosphere. After its birth, 4.5 billion years ago, our planet was subjected to an intense bombardment of meteorites and comets of all sizes. These heavenly bodies contained, in crystalline form, large quantities of water and different gases. From this barrage were born the stone foundations of our planet, as well as the layers of water and air that surround it.

SOURCE: PAUL J. CRUTZEN AND VEERABHADRAN RAMANATHAN, "THE ASCENT OF ATMOSPHERIC SCIENCES," *Science*, 13 OCTOBER 2001, P. 299–304.

Without neglecting other problems, we must focus our attention on this major issue and try to find solutions.

Before concluding this chapter, let me cite one significant piece of evidence that attests to man's influence on the atmosphere. For three days after September 11, 2001, planes were grounded. By comparison with the past, it was shown that the vapour trails left by aircraft in the sky caused a significant reduction in the difference between maximum temperatures for day and night.[22]

2

WHAT ENERGIES FOR TOMORROW?

THE LIMITS OF GROWTH

My first encounter with the problem of global energy consumption goes back to the end of the 1950s. One of our teachers, Philip Morrison, a physics professor at Cornell University in the United States, came in, furious, brandishing a copy of the *New York Times*: "These economists are totally out to lunch: they rave about the wonderful, sustained rise in the nation's gross national product. At this rate, they say, we'll double our energy consumption worldwide in less than ten years. They don't seem to realize that at that rate we'd consume as much energy as the sun in 150 years, and in a thousand years, as much as all the galaxies in the universe!"

In 1970, the Club of Rome published a book called *The Limits of Growth* that attracted a lot of attention. It delivered in a few words the same message as that of my physics professor: resources are not infinite, and humanity will exhaust them within a finite period of time. Exponential growth cannot be tolerated when you have a limited resource.[1]

Fortunately, thanks in part to the oil crisis of 1973–1974, the consumption of energy has not proceeded at a breakneck pace. It took thirty years to double between 1970 and 2000, and should double again in fifty years, by 2050.

The depletion of the planet's energy resources remains a problem, however, and it is becoming more and more a matter of concern. The end time foreseen by the Club of Rome is coming dangerously close in many sectors.

The image of nuclear reactors along our waterways will help us picture the situation. The average power of a reactor is about one billion watts. The current total consumption of energy corresponds to what could be produced by fourteen thousand nuclear reactors. It also corresponds to about fourteen billion electric heaters in our houses, or two heaters per person. These figures, while approximate, will be useful for our discussions.

We expect the world demand for energy to double between now and the middle of the century, due in part to the growing prosperity of a number of countries, such as those in Southeast Asia. Given this demand, there are three possibilities, each with its limitations and its problems.

1. To continue to use fossil energy — oil, gas, coal — which has reserves that will likely exhaust themselves within a century or two, and which, in the meantime, will raise the global temperature through the emission of carbon dioxide.
2. To become more reliant on nuclear energy, which has the advantage of not producing CO_2, but has other significant drawbacks, knowing that to extend these reserves beyond this century, the

industry will require enormous investment at costs difficult to evaluate. As I will discuss later, this should at best be a temporary solution to be abandoned as soon as possible.

3 To rapidly develop renewable energies so that they may assume responsibility for a large proportion of humanity's needs, even though we are still a long way from what would be required.

But before examining each of these options in detail, we must underline a fourth solution, the surest and the least expensive by far: economizing energy. It's not a question of going back in time and illuminating our houses with candles. The energy needed for a comfortable human life — heat, cleanliness, transport, manufactured products —

ENERGY AND POWER UNITS OF MEASUREMENT

Power is energy exerted for one second. The unit of power is the watt (W). Examples: a 100-watt bulb, a 1-kilowatt heater (kW=1,000 watts). A nuclear reactor generates about 1 gigawatt of power (GW=1 billion watts). The human body gives off about 100 W of heat in infrared rays.

The global power used today is about 14,000 GW, or 14 terawatts (TW) (1 TW = 1,000 GW or 1 million MW or 1 billion kW).

The unit of energy is the joule (J). It corresponds to a power of 1 W during one second.

The kilowatt hour (kWh) is one unit of energy, which costs you about five cents Canadian on your electricity bill. It represents the energy generated by a 1,000 watt (1 kW) heater during one hour, or 3 million joules: 3 megajoules (MJ).

We will also employ the energy unit terawatt year (TWy), the equivalent of 10 billion tonnes of oil.

At present, our energy is drawn from the following sources: 74% fossil energy (oil, gas, coal), 6% nuclear, and 20% renewable (hydraulic, biomass, solar, wind).

SOURCE: *Nature*, 1 NOVEMBER 2002, P. 981.

---

is akin to that given off by a modest heater that is always turned on, or 1 kilowatt.

Today, Canada and the United States use twelve times that number, and Western Europe, five times more, while a third of humanity lies well below that norm.

It's this overconsumption we will have to reduce in order to moderate those demands for energy that weigh more and more heavily on our future, and to achieve a more equal distribution of what the world has to offer. All technical progress in the field of energy will be inadequate if we do not first reach this goal.

PLANNING FOR THE LONG TERM

Before addressing this issue, we must situate it in a temporal context. In that way we can avoid those short-sighted policies that have so often been the lot of humanity. Such policies mortgage the future and leave it up to our descendants to pay the price, long-term, for mistakes that could have been avoided if we'd thought ahead.

First, a personal anecdote. At the request of French president, François Mitterrand, Commander Jacques Cousteau set up a group, in which I participated, to defend the rights of future generations. During a government meeting to which we had been summoned, we were asked a question: "What will be tomorrow's energy?" We replied, "What do you mean by 'tomorrow'? Ten years, a hundred years, a thousand years?" No one deigned to reply. It was as though the question were absurd or irrelevant.

The sun will live another five billion years, which theoretically gives humanity a long life expectancy, although other natural hazards could intervene. Let us recall, to put things in perspective, that hominoids appeared over five million years ago, that more than twenty thousand years have elapsed since the time of the Lascaux Cave painters, and that the pharaohs built their pyramids more than four thousand years ago. In this chapter, we will look successively at the short-term (decades, centuries), the medium-term (thousands of years), and the long-term future (millions of years and more).

MAN AND HIS ENERGIES

It might be useful to shift our perspective and to look at the types of energy used by humans since prehistory. I was very moved when I visited a grotto where human beings had lived for almost a million years. The ground in this spot, at Quinson in the French Alpes-de-Haute-Provence, is made up of superimposed layers of refuse deposited by generations that have set foot there. Archaeological excavations reveal vertically the strata corresponding to different periods of occupation.

What is remarkable is that the layers of soil are pale grey in the deeper section, and dark grey beyond a certain time line, corresponding to about four hundred thousand years. The reason: the mastering of fire. These residues contain the ashes of the first hearths. It is impressive is to see the evidence, in the altered colour of the layers, of that crucial point in the history of humankind. For the first time, human beings had mastered a source of energy that brought them comfort.

With the increase in population, a negative factor creeps in bit by bit: deforestation, especially critical in regions where the climate is dry. One need only compare today's barren Mediterranean islands to Homer's descriptions of them in *The Odyssey*, covered in lush green forests. Hannibal captured elephants in the south of Tunisia, then rich in trees. History reminds us that human activity is not the only culprit; overall climatic change is partly responsible.

Let us now look at the different sources of energy man has drawn upon in the course of history. Wood has been used as fuel for tens of thousands of years. With the development of the first steam engine technology — first in England in the eighteenth century, then everywhere in the world — coal rapidly replaced wood as an energy source.

For the first time, non-renewable energy came into play: fossil fuel. Coal was formed more than two hundred million years ago by the slow decomposition of the immense forests that covered the Earth at that time (appropriately called Carboniferous). Natural gas and oil derive from the same phenomenon.

Coal generates a bit less carbon dioxide than wood, but the atmospheric pollution created by the emission of sulphuric acid and particles of soot intensify greatly where the burning of coal is most highly concentrated.

The development of the transport industry drew on another source of fossil energy: oil. About 1960, its use as an energy source began to exceed that of coal. It is much easier to transport (through pipelines) and pollutes the atmosphere quite a bit less than coal; it gives off less carbon dioxide per unit of energy obtained. Another source of fossil energy rapidly emerged towards the end of the twentieth century: natural gas. It is more efficient than oil, with a greater output of energy, and it is also cleaner.

What is reassuring, as we move towards cleaner alternatives, is that we are gradually abandoning those types of energy production that are most harmful to the atmosphere. We are witnessing successive waves of the decarbonization of energy. Wood generates about ten atoms of carbon for each atom of hydrogen; coal, two of carbon for one of hydrogen; and gas, one of carbon for four of hydrogen. In reality, things are a bit more complicated due to the respective productivity of these sources, but, qualitatively, the carbon/hydrogen ratio is a good indicator of how things have evolved, and clearly points the way to the goal we seek: zero carbon. Not only to preserve the atmosphere from the greenhouse effect, but to do better things with these substances than to burn them. How, for example, will we manufacture plastic when there is no more oil?

Finally, we have nuclear energy. Its origins and its history are appended to this chapter (see Appendix 2.1, p. 71). Nuclear energy began to play an important role after the oil crisis in 1973–1974. It has the immense advantage of generating no, or very little, carbon dioxide. But it causes many other problems.

RESOURCES AND THEIR DEPLETION

Today, we are facing the fact that energy reserves are finite, and that at the rate we are consuming them, they will be rapidly exhausted. Predictions are always dangerous, and we must be careful. According to the experts, however, we can risk the following estimates. Let us first consider the types of energy for which techniques of extraction and use have been well mastered. It is generally agreed that oil, natural gas, and slow neutron nuclear energy (which uses uranium-235 in conventional reactors) will be largely depleted before the end of this century, and coal within two or three centuries. That's in the short term.

Where medium-term energy provision is concerned, we should mention fast neutron nuclear energy (the fission of uranium-238 and of thorium[2]). At the rate at which energy demand increases, it is realistic to assume that these reserves could last one thousand years, but not much more. However, such reactors are a long way from being operational.

For the long term (millions of years) there are, at least in principle, several energy sources that are potentially available and usable, whose reserves are almost infinite:

- Solar energy in all its forms: the direct absorption of light rays or sources derived from the sun (wind, waves, water flow — this energy is called hydraulic).
- Nuclear energy derived from the fusion of hydrogen and helium, as in the sun. However, for technical reasons to be discussed later, it is also severely limited in time.
- The thermal energy stored in our planet.

The problem with these sources is not their lifespan, but their productivity. For them to make a significant contribution to the global demand for energy, all of these techniques will require heavy investment and substantial technological advances. Here, we must ask ourselves what the best choice is. We will return to that question at the end of the chapter.

The depletion of oil has been predicted in the past, and such predictions have always turned out to be invalid, whether because we found huge new deposits, or because we developed more efficient technology for extracting reserves we knew were there, or because prices rose to such a degree that it became profitable to seek out reserves that were hard to access.

Why should it be any different now? Well, today those three scenarios seem less pertinent. Here is what the experts say. Oil geologists have looked everywhere and have made no significant finds since the 1970s. We have spent millions of dollars perfecting our drilling techniques and foresee no significant improvements in the future. (The recent finding in Brazil, Canada, and the Arctic Ocean are not significant on that scale.) Finally, in their opinion, even a huge increase in the price of oil will not change the situation radically.[3]

As for uranium, the depletion of which should occur within a century,[4] it exists in sea water, which we might imagine to be an almost inexhaustible source. The problem is that uranium in the sea is extremely diluted, 3 grams in 1,000 tonnes of water. For it to contribute significantly to world demand, we would have to recover hundreds of millions of tonnes, treating, every second, a quantity of water equivalent to 3,000 times the flow of the Rhône river.[5] It's a pharaonic enterprise that could result in serious water pollution.

The annual production of ocean-borne uranium will probably remain very small, and will have little impact on the anticipated depletion of our nuclear reserves. The same would be true for lithium, an element almost as rare as uranium, but essential to nuclear fusion reactions (D+T).

NUCLEAR ENERGY: THE MIRACLE SOLUTION?

When I arrived at Cornell University in 1956, the first nuclear reactors[6] were making their appearance, and civilian nuclear energy was getting a rapturous reception. One gram of uranium could generate as much energy as a tonne of oil. It was practically free. The end of world poverty was in sight.

Behind this euphoric reaction, there was also a sense of redemption. The physicists, who through their work made the destruction of Nagasaki and Hiroshima and the resulting deaths of over two hundred thousand people possible, would, in a way, redeem themselves by offering the world this marvellous gift. Hans Bethe in particular, who discovered that the stars are huge nuclear reactors, and who helped produce the atomic bomb, worked during this period as a scientific consultant for companies that were feverishly building civilian reactors.

My first contact with the reactor builders did not bode well. A few months before the end of my doctorate thesis, Hans Bethe took me into his office to offer me a job with General Dynamics, a company that was then testing a new type of fast neutron reactor, called a super reactor, which would, in principle, be a hundred times more productive than classical reactors. I was invited to spend a week in Detroit, where the prototype would soon become operational. In the car taking me from the airport into the city, the group of engineers that had come to greet me immediately brought me up-to-date on the situation. The big automobile manufacturers, such as Ford and General Motors, located in suburban Detroit, had a jaundiced view of this type of reactor and already regarded it as high risk. It operated at more than 500°C, using liquid sodium as a coolant. And it was very close to the automobile factories.

These manufacturers had taken legal action against General Dynamics to protest the presence of the reactor. My role, as it was explained to me very clearly, was to act as a scientific consultant, and to make a report stating that there was no risk or danger to the region.

"And if that's not my conclusion, what will happen?" I replied.

"Don't worry, that will certainly be your conclusion."

"Then why bring me here if you're so sure you're right?"

"Because, to convince the court, we need the testimony of a professional nuclear physicist from a big university. You will be our scientific seal of approval."

Although troubled by this attitude, I got to work. At the end of the week, not at all convinced that no accident was possible, I refused to make a favourable report and went home.

The super reactor was nevertheless put into operation. One year later, instability in the cooling system triggered a blockage and a serious breakdown. For a few hours, an evacuation of the city of Detroit was contemplated. Repairs were made, but the highly radioactive reactor was closed, and its site surrounded by barbed wire. Today, this charming island, Saint-Clair, on Lake Erie, once a site for family picnics, is still ominously off-limits.

Despite this incredible experience, for years I continued to believe that civilian nuclear energy was the energy of tomorrow, and that the technical problems would soon be resolved — "wishful thinking" that continues to be the trademark of those promoting nuclear energy. One day, I participated in a contradictory debate on the subject. On the "no" side was Pierre Trudeau, later to be prime minister of Canada. In time, our positions reversed themselves: he went over to the "yes" side, and I gradually found myself in opposition because the problems presented by this type of energy extraction turned out to be much more difficult to resolve than had been anticipated. Little by little, I realized that humanity was giving itself over to a technology that no one knew how to control: neither in the disposal of nuclear waste, nor the consequences of a major accident.

MORTGAGING THE FUTURE

What disturbs me most is the mortgage that nuclear power generation leaves hanging over our children and grandchildren. Between the construction of the reactors, their dismantling, and the neutralization of the nuclear waste, it could linger for centuries.

There is no country in the world today that can be assured of economic and political stability for decades or centuries. The Crash of 1929 revealed the fragility of world economies on a scale that had previously not been experienced. Imagine that in the place of the pyramids, the Egyptians had built reactors, and that in the underground chambers of Giza and Karnak, huge quantities of radioactive material were stored. Who would have taken care of them after the collapse of the Egyptian Empire?

It's the kind of thinking that says we'll get what we can from it now and then let our descendants pay the bill — if they can. The idea that other industries do the same is hardly an acceptable excuse.

NUCLEAR WASTE: STORAGE AND TREATMENT

Let's start with the radioactive nucleus that is the most talked about, the star if you wish, or the demon, plutonium-239, the nightmare core of the nuclear industry since the beginning. It remains active for more than a hundred thousand years. Remember that, on our time scale, it was a hundred thousand years ago that *Homo sapiens* appeared on the planet.

This atom, an early constituent of the Earth, completely disappeared billions of years ago. It came back in December 1940, at the University of California in Berkeley. Glenn Seaborg and his colleagues created plutonium nuclei for the first time by bombarding uranium with heavy hydrogen. By May 1941, they had obtained a half-microgram.

Each reactor creates about 200 kilograms per year. Today, there are more than 1,000 tonnes, and the quantity is increasing by 100 tonnes per year. It is accompanied by a vast cohort of other radioactive nuclei with varying lifespans.

There are two ways to resolve the problem of nuclear waste. We can store it as it is — the American solution — or we can partially destroy it, while extracting additional energy.

The problem with storage is finding a place that is secure enough and, above all, free of any internal volcanic movement, a place where waste can remain confined in groundwater without any risk of leakage or dispersion for almost a hundred thousand years. The difficulties the United States has had convincing scientists to accept the site at Yucca Mountain (the best in the country) shows to what degree the situation is controversial.[7]

As for the second solution, the treatment of waste, there are two possible methods: the use of super reactors[8] or the use of accelerator reactors.[9] These instruments have the dual advantage of greatly increasing the reserves and of making use of the waste accumulated up to that point. But before being able to destroy the waste, one must store it on the surface for decades, even centuries, awaiting a significant drop in its radioactivity.[10] Radioactive discharge into the environment from this method has already been observed, and complaints have been lodged. Of course, the quantities have been small, but if the nuclear industry were to expand its activity in order to respond to the demand for global energy, the situation could become much more dangerous.

Add to the problem of dealing with nuclear waste the dismantling of reactors that have finished their work.[11] Because of the very high radioactivity that prevails within their confines, their lifespan is limited to between thirty and sixty years. Then, one must wait several more decades for the level of radioactivity to drop enough that one may go safely inside. All these operations together, from the construction to the destruction of a reactor, take a century to complete. Which is why we may say that nuclear energy mortgages the future of succeeding generations. It's not enough to argue that our other options are even more threatening.

ACCIDENTS

Although the problems of storing nuclear waste and the construction of nuclear facilities are serious, the potential for accidents is catastrophic. Chernobyl was a brutal awakening to the real and immediate dangers of civilian nuclear energy. It was one of history's great technological disasters. It has caused enormous human and ecological damage. We know that excessive exposure to radioactivity causes leukemia and thyroid cancers. Some writers have talked about the many additional cancers linked in some degree to Chernobyl, but figures are difficult to verify.[12] Professor Yuri Bandazhevsky was condemned to eight years in prison in Russia for having prepared a study on the pathological effects of Chernobyl on children, although the official charge brought against him was that he had accepted bribes from his students' parents. An international movement was formed to have him released, leading to his liberation in 2005.

Before this disaster on April 26, 1986, there was the serious Three Mile Island accident in Pennsylvania in March of 1979, which brought to an abrupt halt the construction of reactors in the United States.

In fact, the frequency of both major and minor accidents has shown itself to be much greater than that predicted at the outset by nuclear statisticians. The reason is simple, and disturbing. They are almost always caused by the operators themselves, not by machines. At Chernobyl, security systems had been disconnected in order to perform certain experiments. No security system, no matter how perfect, can protect us from human error. No program to calculate probabilities can take them into account.[13] The situation is no different in hydroelectric generating plants, where accidents occur as well. Only the consequences are not as grave. For decades, no one has even talked about them.

It has often occurred to me that nuclear technology was not meant for humans, but for angels. For perfect beings, in other words, who (in theory) never make mistakes. Humans are easily distracted, and sometimes confused. Who will prevent a watchman from deserting his post a bit early on a summer evening to go fishing?

There are many other problems associated with the use of atomic energy. I will try to deal with them in order of their gravity.

SECURITY

Where internal security is concerned, the safety record of reactors has greatly improved. The rate of accidents, even minor ones, decreased by a factor of twenty between 1990 and 2000. What is more, new types of safer reactors — with no risk of fusion — are being built, especially in Japan. They are furnished with highly sophisticated security systems that should greatly reduce the risks.

But it's important to repeat again, and very clearly: if nuclear energy were to contribute significantly to our global energy needs from now to the middle of the century, these secure reactors would become unusable for lack of fuel (uranium-235). It's a short-term solution.

We should also remember that the most spectacular errors in the past — Three Mile Island and Chernobyl — were caused by human error. Even if we accept that security measures can protect us from mechanical dysfunction, can we conceive of measures that would be invulnerable to the lapses of human beings? And what guarantee do we have that on the scale of decades and centuries these security systems will be well taken care of? Economic and social crises and wars could bring in their wake a breakdown in maintenance. Just look at the state of the installations in the former Soviet Union.

TERRORISM

The events of September 11, 2001, pointed to another disturbing weakness of nuclear reactors. They are a perfect target for terrorists. The idea of a kamikaze attack on a super reactor is very frightening. A single incident of this type could compromise the entire future of the nuclear industry. However, according to engineers in the field, the fallout would not be as severe as one might expect. Is that reassuring? Probably not. The real disaster would result from the general panic and the human and economic costs of a mass evacuation of the population.

What is more disturbing are the thefts of nuclear material associated with the increase in terrorism. In its annual report for 2000, the International Atomic Energy Agency (IAEA) acknowledged that groups of terrorists or other individuals had tried to steal nuclear materials. The IAEA made clear that the struggle against illicit trafficking had become a priority, as incidents continue to take place. During the two years preceding the report's appearance, four thefts had been reported, the most significant of which involved 920 grams of highly enriched uranium. The IAEA has set up a program that includes the exchange of information, assistance to bodies of control, and training activities. It has also created a database dealing with instances of illicit trafficking.[14]

THE COST OF KILOWATT HOURS

Partisans of nuclear energy often emphasize the reduced cost of this source of energy. The cost of a nuclear kilowatt hour is a notion as flexible as that of the rate of unemployment. It varies depending on who is making the estimate, and the gap between official sources and others is often great. It all depends on what goes into the mix.[15]

In fact, many independent research organizations and energy consultants have concluded that if we take into account the true costs, nuclear energy is much more expensive (and hazardous) than all other types of electricity production. Realistic estimates of the cost per kilowatt hour, factoring in the price of dismantling the reactors and dealing with the waste, frighten off private investors. What is more, insurance companies refuse to insure the reactors.

Which brings up a very significant fact: wherever a competitive energy market exists, very few countries invest in nuclear energy. Companies like British Petroleum and Shell Oil, that sense the end of the oil era, are not investing in nuclear but in renewable energies. There are countries with an energy monopoly — France and some others — that persevere in this path. Result: the total energy generated by reactors has increased less than 6% over the last ten years.

The argument for economic independence is more understandable. We are all at the mercy of Middle East politics. This dependence, which infuriates the United States, is not unconnected to recent wars in the Middle East. But if we take a closer look, the situation is potentially not that different where uranium producers are concerned. According to a report by the European Commission, the countries of the European Union possess only 2% of global reserves. Can we call that energy independence?

The hostility towards nuclear energy within many populations, not to mention the fear that it instills, is certainly an obstacle to the industry's development. The Chernobyl disaster, but also the silences and lies of official agencies — "the cloud stopped at the French border ..." — have played a significant role in the outcry and in the enormous psychological resistance of the public, vis-à-vis a return to nuclear energy. The attempts to reassure people by understating the problems causes the public to turn against the agencies once the entire situation is brought to light. Here is a telling anecdote on that subject. One morning, Camille, my wife, said to me: "There has just been a serious accident in a nuclear generating plant in the USSR. I heard it on an independent radio station. We have to watch the television news." To our great surprise, none of this information was broadcast on television that day, neither at noon, nor in the evening.

Several months later, I met the journalist responsible for the program. He told me the government ordered the silence: "Don't panic the population." Recently, the most important electric company in Japan admitted to having falsified its reactor inspections for ten years. Behaviour like this goes a long way towards explaining why people are so suspicious of nuclear energy. Omissions and lies — nuclear history is full of them — leave their mark.

In certain quarters, nuclear power was close to being demonized. The close ties between the civilian and military sectors contributed to this, even when it was asserted that the new reactors could in no way produce material for use in bombs. How could the public have confidence in such a declaration? Any attempt to restart the industry risks enormous resistance. This phobia, however irrational it may be, is in fact one of the major obstacles in pursuing nuclear programs within democracies.

THE NUCLEAR COMEBACK

People, however, are talking more and more about reviving the construction of nuclear facilities. Many think we must develop both new nuclear technology and renewable energy.[16]

In March of 2001, the Bush administration decided to revive the nuclear option. The Nuclear Power 2010 project's goal is the construction of new generators between now and the end of the decade. In Europe, Finland is building a new reactor, and the British seem to be leaving the door open to new nuclear investment. These reactors are conventional slow neutron reactors that use light uranium (235), the reserves of which, remember, will not survive the century.

In the medium term, this revival of the nuclear option will only satisfy the demand if we find a way to extract energy from heavy uranium (238) as well as thorium. But we already know that getting these operations off the ground will require costly investment and major development.

Exercise all of our options? Fine. But we need realistic cost projections, and we have to evaluate the risks involved in each technology; above all, we must not mortgage the future for centuries, if not millennia. We will return to this point at the end of the chapter.

RENEWABLE ENERGIES

Let's turn now to renewable energies. We will stick to this term, which has now become part of the language, even though I prefer "inexhaustible energies."

First of all, there is solar energy. One hundred and fifty million kilometres distant, our yellow star boasts attributes that are very moderate compared to other stars in the Milky Way.

The Earth continually receives and absorbs energy equivalent to a hundred million nuclear generators — about ten thousand times the quantity we require to satisfy humanity's current needs. In other words, our annual demand corresponds to all the incident solar energy received by a country the size of Belgium.

To harvest it, must we cover an equally large surface with solar panels? Fortunately not. Many natural phenomena are able to concentrate that energy: the evaporation of water, the photosynthesis of plants (biomass), the wind, the waves, and water currents. Winds and water currents owe their existence to the fact that the polar regions receive less solar energy than those nearer the equator. The temperature difference generates permanent air and water circulation between these regions. The Earth's rotation interferes with these movements and gives rise to air vortexes (the cyclones and anticyclones so familiar to those who watch weather reports) and to ocean currents such as the Gulf Stream.

Today, hydroelectric generators are the principal harvesters of solar energy. Rain evaporates from the oceans, falls back into the mountains, and flows down as streams of water. Held back by dams, it drives turbines that produce electricity. Today, these potential energy sources are already in full use in many countries, and not much more can be expected of them in the future. We'll need other options.

Windmills (*Figures 2.1 and 2.2*) represent one of the most profitable energy sources.[17] This technology has the wind in its sails, so to speak, and is increasing at a rate of 40% per year. According to some (perhaps optimistic) studies, it could, by 2050, satisfy 10 to 20% of the world's electrical needs.

There are drawbacks. Windmills present problems of energy storage, but significant technological advances are being reported all over the world. Detractors often focus on the aesthetic problem. "These huge constructions, sometimes a hundred metres high, are a blot on the landscape!"

This remark leads me to a more general observation. Every energy source comes with its own problems. Hydroelectric dams flood vast territories and alter the landscape. Biomass on a large scale could compromise biodiversity. But between carbon dioxide, nuclear waste, and these problems, we have to make a choice.

To return to the windmills, a popular solution today is to situate them at sea. There are two advantages to this: they are less visible, and the wind blows harder there. Along the coast of England, three-hundred-

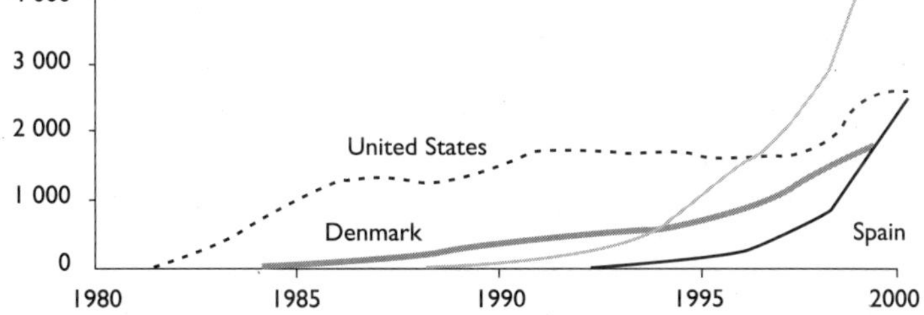

Figure 2.1. Increase in the energy capacity of windmills since 1980 in the most active regions.

SOURCE: *Vital Signs*, 2001, P. 45.

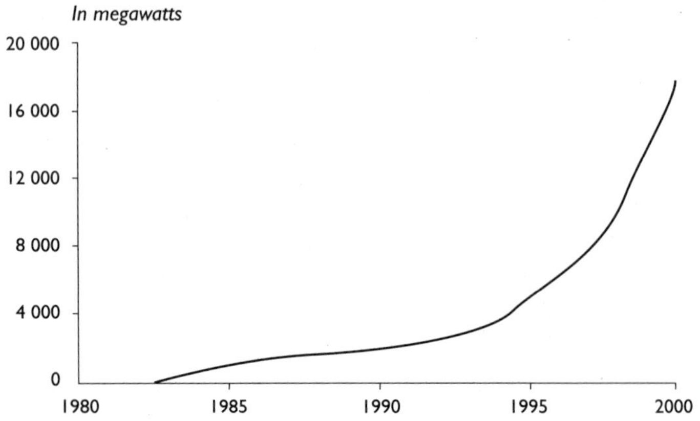

Figure 2.2. Increase in the energy capacity of windmills the world over since 1980.
SOURCE: *Vital Signs*, 2001, P. 45.

metre-high towers are planned, which could deliver one-third of the electrical requirements of that country.

There are other ways of extracting solar energy.

The natural method is the photosynthesis of green plants. Plants mix water and carbon dioxide with air to produce vegetal substances, and give off oxygen. On a global scale, energy produced by the combustion of trees could reliably provide us with energy equivalent to that of ten reactors. What is more, by burning household garbage and agricultural residue (straw), globally, we could produce energy equivalent to many more additional reactors. The CO_2 given off by this operation was formerly taken out of the atmosphere by plant growth.[18] The net balance: no additional CO_2.

Finally, solar energy may be transformed into an electric current directly through the photoelectric process used in solar panels[19] (*Figure 2.3*). Solar heating and electrification for homes are being actively developed in a number of countries. Solar towers and even satellites that would capture solar energy are being devised.

Year	Production (in megawatts)
1980	7
1981	8
1982	9
1983	17
1984	22
1985	23
1986	26
1987	29
1988	34
1989	40
1990	46
1991	55
1992	58
1993	60
1994	69
1995	79
1996	89
1997	126
1998	153
1999	201
2000	288

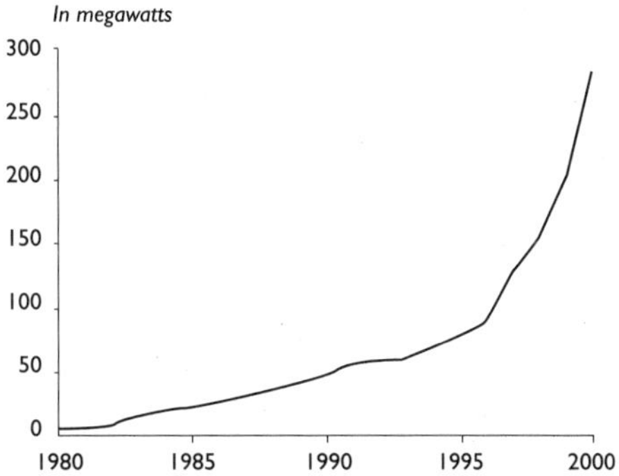

Figure 2.3. Energy production since 1980 through photovoltaic technology (solar panels).
SOURCE: *Vital Signs*, 2001, P. 47.

HYDROGEN

Hydrogen is often talked about as a future energy source. Be we must take care, as this word can cause confusion. The word "hydrogen" is used in two completely different contexts.

There is, on the one hand, the fusion of hydrogen and helium, as in the sun and the hydrogen bomb. This energy is nuclear; it is generated by atomic nuclei. We'll discuss it further on.

On the other hand, there is the combination of hydrogen and oxygen to make water, as in space rockets. This energy is atomic as it is generated by the combination of atoms and molecules.

Another important difference: the combination of hydrogen and water only gives back the energy we have expended by separating water and hydrogen in the first place. In that respect, it is not primary energy, like oil, but secondary energy. It does not increase the amount of energy available to us, it just enables us to distribute it differently. Over great distances, the transportation of hydrogen is less costly than that of electricity, and we could also use it for cars and buses. Some hydrogen-fuelled cars could be commercially available in a few years.

In all these areas, constant progress is being made, and unexpected breakthroughs make it difficult to realistically estimate the amount of time needed to achieve commercialization. In fact, it's all a question of political will and economic means. Even if efforts are being made, our unfortunate tendency to think short-term holds us back from mustering large-scale resources.

Ten years ago, after a lecture I gave to engineers from the organization Environmental Defence, I asked them why they had abandoned their development work on the Odeillo experiment in the Pyrenees — a huge mirror designed to capture the sun's rays. Their reply, word for word: "It wasn't profitable compared to oil." I answered that if there are still men on Earth in a few thousand years, which is what we hope, oil and nuclear reserves will have been depleted for a long time, and solar energy will certainly be playing a crucial role. Their work today would have laid the groundwork for its profitability. "Yes, of course," they replied, vaguely amused. This seemed to me to be a typically irresponsible case in point. The absence of long-term thinking can only have negative consequences.

CONTROLLED HYDROGEN FUSION (D+T REACTION)

Hydrogen is the energy source for the sun and the stars. Four atoms of hydrogen are combined by nuclear force to produce helium through a proton-proton reaction. The mass of one atom of helium is inferior, by about 1%, to the combined mass of the four hydrogen atoms. The difference is emitted in the form of heat (the famous equation $E = mc^2$).

Such a reaction can only occur at very high temperatures or very high density. At the centre of the sun, it is fifteen million °C. The reason is simple: protons (the nuclei of hydrogen atoms) charged electrically, repel each other, except when they are brought close enough together for the nuclear attraction to override the electrostatic repulsion. They have to practically touch. They then fuse and form helium nuclei, generating energy.

Since the sun runs on nuclear fusion, we could follow its example in tapping a source of energy. Indeed, we've succeeded in exploding H-bombs in Bikini, Mururoa, and Novaya Zemlya, Siberia.

The easiest way to obtain this result on Earth is by the fusion of a nucleus of deuterium (heavy hydrogen) with a nucleus of tritium (even heavier hydrogen), usually called the D+T reaction.

We know how to produce, briefly, the appropriate conditions in laboratories; we have reached fifty million °C for a few microseconds. The problem is to maintain these conditions and have them last long enough that we can extract a significant amount of energy. No solid substance — metal or ceramic — can remain stable beyond a few thousand degrees.

An early technique was "fusion by magnetic confinement," or Tokamak, the name of a Russian prototype. The idea was to create magnetic "cages" in which the hydrogen atoms remain trapped at very high temperatures long enough for the transformation to take place. But the cages are not completely leak-proof, and the problems of leakage complicate the situation enormously. More secure prototypes have been devised over the last few decades. The progress is real, transformations have succeeded, but the energy generated by the manipulation remains far inferior to that which could be obtained by fission. For the option to be commercially viable, the energy generated would, of course, have to be much higher.

This project, after many setbacks, seems to have been given a new lease on life with the development of a new instrument called ITER (International Thermonuclear Experimental Reactor), a product of international collaboration. The laboratory is already under construction at Cadarache in the south of France.

The United States and France are also interested in a second hydrogen and helium fusion technique called "inertial fusion." Here, empty shells of heavy hydrogen ice (deuterium and tritium), a few millimetres in dimension, are violently compressed by powerful laser beams for a few billionths of a second. The density can reach four hundred times that of water, and the pressure a billion times that of the atmosphere. Fusion takes place, but the energy obtained still represents only about a millionth of the energy invested. For it to become operational, it would have to be twenty times greater.

Controlled fusion with hydrogen would be a very desirable type of energy production: no transportation of radioactive waste, no risk of snowballing, sixty times more energy produced per gram than is produced by fission, and no possible military application. But the drawbacks would also be many. As the reactors would be bombarded by very active neutrons (14 MeV) generated by the reaction, their lifespan would be comparable to that of fission reactors. They would also have to be dismantled, with all of the problems that involves.

Another difficulty with this technique is the problem of leakage. Tritium, a radioactive-heavy hydrogen used in this process, has a life of twelve years and easily passes through walls and escapes into the countryside.

What is more, tritium does not exist freely in nature; we obtain it from lithium, an element almost as rare as uranium, and whose resources are also very limited. The world reserves are evaluated at twelve million tonnes — quite comparable to the uranium reserve. In other words, controlled fusion achieved with tritium is far from being an inexhaustible energy source.

NUCLEAR FUSION: THE D+D REACTON

The only fusion reaction that would appear to be appropriate for our energetic needs for the long term is the fusion of two deuterium nuclei (D+D). The reserve (ocean water) is inexhaustible. The problem however is that it is much more difficult than D+T and would require the attainment of many hundred millions of degrees in the lab. Many experts in the field consider the realization of this source of energy on an industrial scale as totally unrealistic. Who knows? But to remain in a realistic frame for our discussion, it appears advisable to forget this source. And consider that nuclear energy is in the same situation as petrol; on the time scale of the human species, it is totally inadequate.

The ideal reaction for achieving controlled fusion would be the bombardment of boron nuclei (isotope-11) with protons, producing carbon-12 nuclei, without neutrons but with gamma rays, which are easier to control. But we would require temperatures of hundreds of millions of degrees — an extremely distant goal. And boron is just as rare as lithium.

THE EARTH'S INNER WARMTH

One might ask whether we will eventually discover other sources of energy. After all, science moves on and new discoveries are continually being made. It's not impossible, but it's not at all certain that new forms of energy will be found in the near or distant future. But it seems to me that it would not be wise to count on it too much. It's escapism, once again. We must avoid leaving the burden of finding solutions to our current problems to the future. We can only rely on the present.

As for the Earth's much talked about inner warmth, some of this heat source has already been drawn upon, in Iceland and Germany for example. Similarly, the massive harnessing of tides, ocean currents, and waves is actively being pursued.

WHAT IS TO BE DONE?

We are, therefore, living in a very delicate period, where we must juggle three conflicting imperatives simultaneously: we must continue to satisfy human energy needs, we must significantly reduce emissions of carbon dioxide, and we must avoid the problems associated with nuclear energy.

While awaiting the transition to renewable energy, the slow neutron nuclear generator is certainly a lesser evil than an increase in the greenhouse effect. But as the Swedes say, "We must get rid of them as soon as possible." Our first priority is to stop the increase in temperature and avoid the disastrous scenarios described in the prologue.

Important decisions have to be made regarding the long-term future. Our leaders talk with reason about the need to diversify our energy sources. Again, remember that slow neutron nuclear resources will be exhausted in less than a century, and, that in order for it to be put into effect, fast neutron nuclear energy requires significant technological developments and considerable investment.

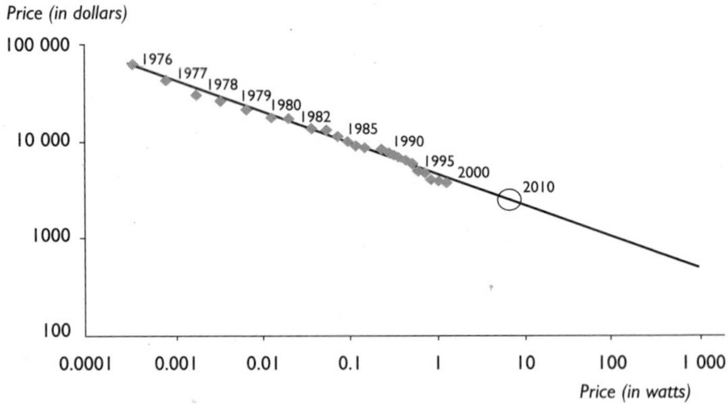

Figure 2.4. Decrease in the average price of photovoltaic modules (in 1999 American dollars per watt) since 1976. On the ordinate axis: the average price of a photovoltaic module divided by its maximum power as a function of the total power generated by all the modules sold. The price falls 20% every time sales double.

The problems with renewable energy are different. Excellent techniques already exist, even if research is still required to improve their effectiveness. It's, above all, a question of the cost per kilowatt hour. The more widespread its use, the more the costs will go down, due to the large-scale manufacturing of its components. And for that, government help is needed, for example, in the form of grants for the purchase of components and of electricity by Environmental Defence at advantageous prices.

NIMBY AND NIMTO

The minimum [of actions, expenses, investments] that is scientifically necessary [to combat global warming] far exceeds the maximum that is politically feasible.
AL GORE, 2000

These two American expressions sum up one of the most serious aspects of tomorrow's energy problems. NIMBY means "not in my backyard," and NIMTO, "not in my term of office." We are touching here on the problem of citizens' resistance to the solutions being proposed to stop global warming.

The revival of super generators, which would involve the construction of thousands of new reactors, plus the need to find places to store nuclear waste ("not in my backyard"), risk spawning very stubborn opposition (all the more powerful, given that the emotional implications are so great). In the face of this, even the most determined ministers are likely to back off ("not in my term of office"). To impose measures by decree could be even more politically disastrous. The likely result of this public opposition is that decisions will be put off until fossil fuels are exhausted.

The resistance to renewable solutions, also real (the NIMBY campaign against windmills), will likely be much less intense. That is one more concrete reason to favour the solar over the nuclear.

CONCLUSION: WE MUST LEARN FROM THE PAST. WE MUST NOT MAKE THE SAME MISTAKES.

At the beginning of the twentieth century, humanity threw itself body and soul into the exploitation of oil. We made oil the key element in our development and industry, acting as though this resource (just like coal and natural gas) was inexhaustible. Today it has become clear to us that we are reaching "the bottom of the barrel."

Let us not make the same mistake with nuclear energy (uranium, thorium, and indirectly with lithium for the deuterium-tritium reaction). These resources are limited as well, and the bottom of the barrel is never far off on the time scales that interest us here. Meeting our energy demands and their probable growth would exhaust them in a few centuries, in a few thousand years at the very least. (The only resource that might exceed this limit is the fusion of two deuterium nuclei, whose economic viability, according to the best experts, remains a utopian dream.)

Clearly, if there are still people on Earth in a few thousand years, they will be using solar and/or geothermic energy. If such matters had been kept in mind at the time of the first oil crisis (1972), this is the path that would have been taken, rather than our embarking upon the construction of nuclear reactors. We would then have avoided all the problems and dramas associated with that technology (Chernobyl, Three Mile Island, nuclear waste, and so on).

We too easily forget that humanity has existed on our planet for hundreds of thousands of years, and that it is our responsibility to ensure that it can continue to do so for a long time to come.

Appendix

2.1 THE ORIGINS AND HISTORY OF NUCLEAR ENERGY

Interstellar space contains a large variety of radioactive atoms such as uranium and plutonium. Created in the interior of stars, they are scattered throughout space when the stars die. After a specific time for each type, these atoms break down on their own. They separate into several pieces in a process called "fission," which generates a lot of energy. When our solar system was formed 4.5 billion years ago, the nebula from which it was born contained a small fraction of uranium, thorium, and other radioactive atoms handed down from generations of earlier stars.

The stones that represent the Earth's rocky foundations inherited a certain quantity of radioactive atoms with vastly different life expectancies. An aluminum isotope (aluminum-26) with a lifetime of about a million years played a particularly crucial role in the warming of the primitive Earth. Its disintegration endowed the heart of our planet with an initial heat that, since that time, has slowly radiated towards the surface and into space, causing movement that is responsible for continental drift, volcanic eruptions, and earthquakes, but also gas emissions that, for billions of years, enabled the Earth to maintain a temperature above 0°C, and enabled water to remain liquid, as we established earlier on.

This heat also allowed for the settling of chemical elements. Iron and some other elements may be found in the centre of the planet, while a large number of others, including silicon and uranium, are embedded in the higher layers. Since this period, the radioactive elements have been decreasing in number at their own pace.

Because of their long lifetimes, the uranium and thorium found in the Earth's crust have not entirely broken down. One need only place one's hand on these stones to feel the heat thrown off by the disintegration. Significant concentrations remain in mineral form, which today we extract in specific mines.

The radioactive properties of uranium were discovered in 1900 by Henri Becquerel. Some years later, Marie Curie brought to light the existence of a number of radioactive elements (uranides) produced by the disintegration of uranium and thorium. About 1936, a very important property of these uranides was discovered: the possibility of accelerating their disintegration by bombarding them with neutrons (induced disintegration), and later, the possibility of chain reactions (in disintegrating, the uranium nuclei eject neutrons, which can, in turn, trigger the disintegration of other nuclei, etc.) These successive fissions can generate an enormous amount of energy. The operation gave rise to two different applications: atomic bombs and nuclear reactors.

The basic difference between civilian and military nuclear applications is a matter of dosage. In reactors, the rate of the reaction is controlled. The reactor's properties are adjusted to ensure that the reactions proceed at a regular pace. For a bomb, we accelerate to the maximum. The energy is given off in a brief instant.

3

WHAT ARE WE GOING TO EAT TONIGHT?

Forests precede peoples,
deserts come after them.
François-René de Chateaubriand

A TROUBLING QUESTION.

I'd first like to cite Woody Allen in *Hannah and Her Sisters*. "There are four big questions: Where do we come from? Who are we? Where are we going? And what are we going to eat tonight?" The question becomes all the more pertinent if the night in question is in 2050.

One point must be made from the outset: the disastrous population explosion so often forecast is not really happening. A shift is already evident almost everywhere on the planet.[1] There is good reason to think that the world population, today about 6.6 billion, will stabilize around the middle of the century at about eight or ten billion (See "The Growth in Human Population," p. 75) (*Figures 3.1 and 3.2*).

According to some, it could even shrink significantly beyond that, due to the planet's deterioration and the effects of certain toxins on the human capacity to reproduce (*See Prologue, Note 15*). We no longer have cause, therefore, to fear an exponential population growth that will deplete food resources and fresh water within a few decades.

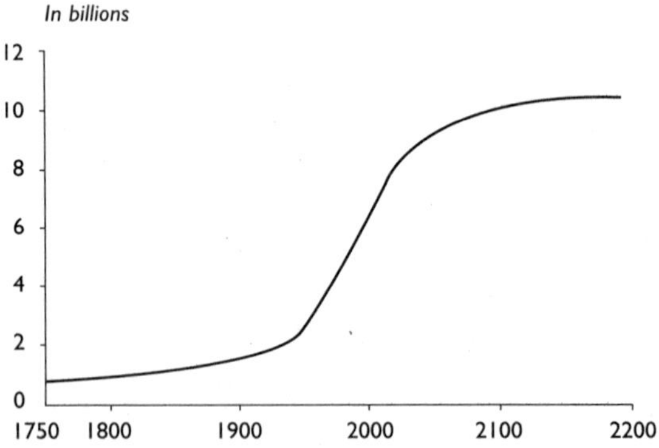

Figure 3.1. The world's population from 1750 to 2200 (UN estimate).

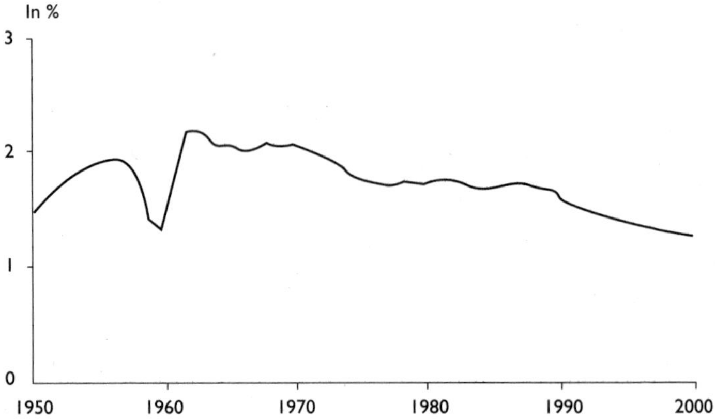

Figure 3.2. Variation in the annual growth rate of the world's population. After a maximum of 2.2% during the 1960s, the rate has dropped to less than 1.5%, leading us to foresee a stabilization of the global population (today 6.6 billion) at about 8 to 10 billion inhabitants around the middle of the twenty-first century.

SOURCE: *Vital Signs*, 2002, P. 89.

THE GROWTH IN HUMAN POPULATION

Here are a few figures from various sources. Bear in mind that estimates concerning the distant past are difficult to make and should be taken with caution.

Two million years ago, the population of hominoids on Earth was about ten thousand. Ten thousand years ago it had reached ten million, doubtlessly due to the significant growth in foodstuffs generated by animal breeding and agriculture.

From three hundred million at the time of the Roman Empire, the population rose to eight hundred million at the start of the Industrial Era (1750). From that point on, we observe a new acceleration linked to technical innovation; 1 billion in 1800; 1.7 billion in 1900; 2.5 billion in 1950; 4 billion in 1978; 6 billion in 2000.

The rapid acceleration after the Second World War was due to vaccination and a better-fed population. Since 1960–1970, the population has tended to stabilize, probably due to urbanization, education for women, and contraception, but also because of AIDS *(twenty million dead). The maximum growth took place in 1988, with 8.6 million additional inhabitants. In 1998 there were 7.8 million. The annual growth rate has gone from 2% in 1960 to about 1.2% in 2000.*

There is an 85% probability that the global population will stop growing before 2100, and a 60% probability that it will not exceed ten billion.

SOURCE: *Nature*, 2 AUGUST 2001.

Let us deal first with the question of food. For some time now, hunger has become less of a problem. Beyond certain regions of Africa and India that are still, as a consequence of political ideology, subject to endemic famine, the great food shortages that afflicted humanity throughout its history have begun to diminish. The stockpiles set aside by international organizations, rapidly flown in, enable us to face up to crisis situations such as storms, earthquakes, and flights of refugees.

The famines that were predicted in the middle of the twentieth century and predicated on a rapid increase in the Earth's population did not take place at the century's end, thanks to the green revolution. Scientific studies of plant growth and the development of a technology that uses nitrogen fertilizer effectively, have increased harvests almost everywhere around the globe. Between 1950 and 2000, the world production of cereals — the principal product of arable land — rose from 600 to 1,900 million tonnes, or from 250 to 300 kilograms per person, which represents a more rapid growth than that of the population. The yield of maritime fishing went from twenty million to ninety million tonnes between 1950 and 1998. The growth in fishing was double the population growth, even if it now accounts for only 7% of world food consumption. In short, hunger in the world has been reduced to what is probably its lowest level in history.

We still count, however, more than a billion human beings, or one out of six, who live an extremely precarious existence and do not have enough to eat.

We can only deplore the scandalous North-South gap, and the disparity in wealth (we'll return to this issue at some length in Chapter 6), because it's a crucial problem for the planet's future. In the two world regions where people are still affected by chronic famine — India and sub-Saharan Africa — the causes are the same: significant population growth and weak agricultural production linked to problems of aridity, drought, and a lack of water.

As long as this population problem is not solved, no enduring solution will be found in these regions. But hunger would still exist in many other parts of the world if we had not seen this boom in agricultural productivity thanks to the technological revolution. Over the last twenty years, East Asia and Latin America have almost totally overcome the curse of hunger. In China, for example, the proportion of the population suffering from malnutrition has decreased from 30% in 1980 to 10% in 2000.

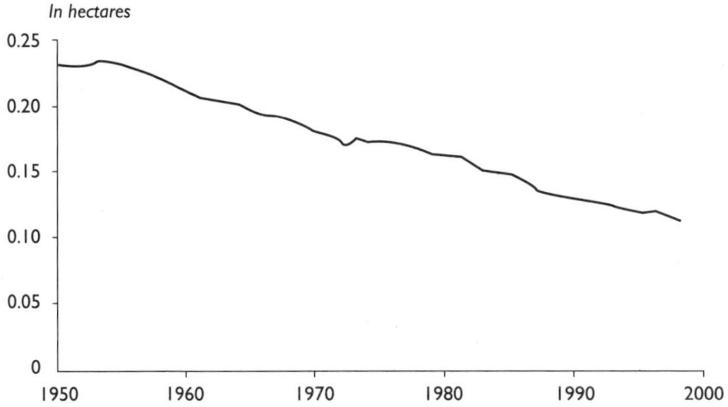

Figure 3.3. The area dedicated to the cultivation of cereals per global inhabitant declined from 0.23 hectares in 1950 to 0.12 hectares in 2000.

SOURCE: *Vital Signs*, 1999, P. 43.

Will this situation last? That is the question. What we must ask ourselves today is whether we will be able to respond to the food requirements of a population that will likely continue to grow until 2050. There are several reasons for us to be uneasy. For some years, since about 1995, the green revolution has shown signs of fatigue. The world production of cereals began to decline in 1984, falling from 342 kilograms to 308 kilograms per person between 1984 and 2000.[2]

To nourish populations that are continuing to grow, we must increase production considerably. Present quotas already depend on an exploitation of land and water that is not sustainable. We are using more than half our reserves of fresh water. We are living on our capital rather than on our interest, and that is not healthy.[3] The gravity of the situation shows itself in many ways.

One of the most worrying aspects is the shrinking of arable land — land one can cultivate. More than 60,000 square kilometres of arable land (representing a surface area equal to that of Belgium and the Netherlands together) is disappearing every year (*Figure* 3.3). The causes vary. Rapid urbanization, including the development of industrial zones and road networks, is obliterating much of our fertile land, especially near large cities in places like China and Mexico.

Add to that soil pollution caused by intensive cultivation. To increase their yields, growers use more and more fertilizer, pesticides, and water (*Figure* 3.4). Chemical fertilizers make the soil more compact and more vulnerable to drought and erosion. Nitrates infiltrate coastal waters, where they destroy significant numbers of fish. Irrigation results in the massive evaporation of water, leaving a deposit of salts that makes the soil sterile.

Vast regions of Pakistan have become desert. Between 1980 and 1998, Kazakhstan, one of the great grain producers, lost half of its arable land due to wind erosion. The Gobi desert continues to spread at the expense of pasture land, due to the depletion of groundwater. In Haiti, half the arable land has disappeared. By 2020, the populated regions of Asia will have no more arable land to spare. Just about everywhere, we are witnessing the land's impoverishment (*Figure* 3.5).

Desertification is progressing at an extremely fast pace. In 1980, a third of the continents' surface was desert. It's expected that this fraction will rise to 40% by 2010, and perhaps to 50% by 2020.

What is more, the global climatic disturbances referred to at the beginning of the book could have disastrous consequences for food production. The rise in sea level could cause flooding of low-lying lands where rice is cultivated, especially in Asia.

NITRATES

We are now facing negative fallout from that same green revolution that made an extraordinary upsurge in agricultural production possible. The problems are attributable to chemical fertilizer and pesticides, which are responsible for serious pollution and the impoverishment of the soil.

Let us first look at nitrates. Nitrogen is a gas that constitutes 70% of the air we breathe. But unlike oxygen, it is not absorbed by the lungs.

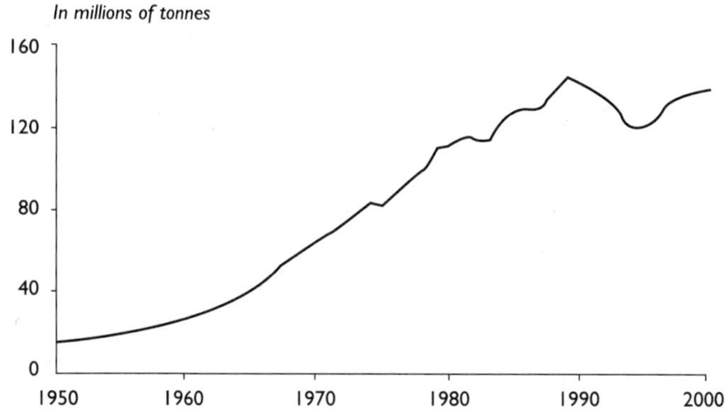

Figure 3.4. Increase in the quantity of fertilizer used since 1950.

SOURCE: *Vital Signs*, 2001, P. 33.

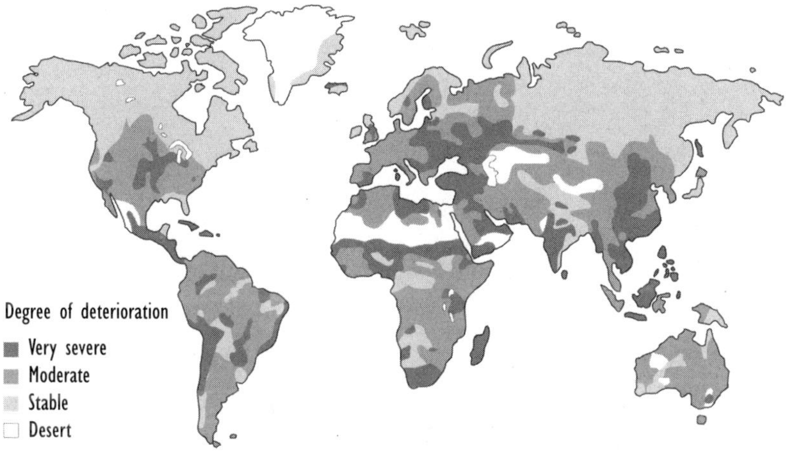

Figure 3.5. The deterioration of the world's land, through over-grazing, deforestation, over-irrigation, etc. Arable territory is steadily dwindling.

In fact, its name in French, *azote*, means "without life." However, nitrogen is an element essential to life's chemical structuring. We find it in every cell of our body in various forms, including that of DNA, our genetic molecules.

For it to reach living organisms, nitrogen is first extracted from the soil by the roots of certain nitrifying plants, such as potatoes. It is a slow and rather complex process that involves a symbiosis between the roots of these plants and particular fungi. After a few years, during which other plants without this property have been cultivated, the soil is depleted of nitrate and becomes sterile. It has to be nitrified all over again with nitrifying plants.

In 1912, the German chemists Haber and Bosch discovered that it was possible to manufacture synthetic fertilizer in the laboratory. From nitrogen and air, they produced a molecule called "ammonium nitrate" that plants could absorb directly. There followed a rapid increase in yields.

There was a problem, however. Plants treated in this way sometimes absorb only 10% of the fertilizer, with 90% being released into the environment. The atoms of nitrogen remain reactive for a long time and produce a number of harmful chemical compounds: nitrates that poison the soil and the groundwater, nitric acid, which causes acid rain, and nitrogen oxides, which are greenhouse gases. Today, the global production of synthetic nitrates exceeds the natural production by nitrifying plants and risks increasing even more thanks to the countries of South Asia, where rapid fertilization is essential.[4]

PESTICIDES

The first pesticides, like DDT, were introduced in the 1940s, and made a big difference to the harvests.[5] But ten years later, the first pesticide-resistant insects appeared. We used other pesticides, with the same results. As with antibiotics, we found ourselves in a race.

Now, it is commonly said that insects learn to resist pesticides. In fact, it's not that the insects learn to resist, but rather, in a given population, there is a tiny minority that is not affected. This population then increases to the detriment of others. It's a typical example of life's adaptive capacities, natural selection as Darwin observed. The number of pesticide-resistant species exceeds a thousand, including about five hundred insect species, and the figure has been growing since 1940 (*Figure 3.6*).

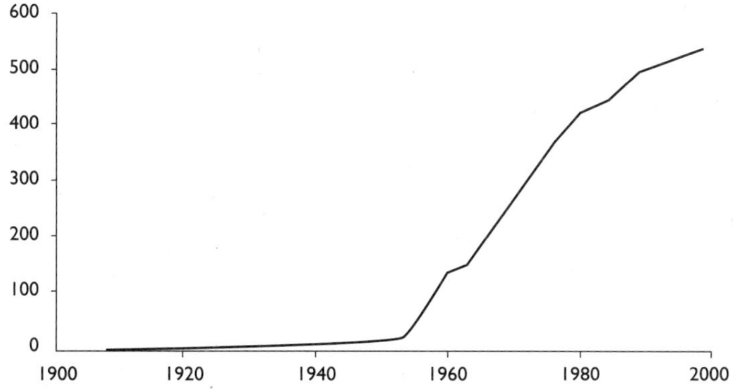

Figure 3.6. The number of species resistant to pesticides, since 1908.
SOURCE: *Vital Signs*, 1999, P. 124.

The drawbacks of pesticides are many, and are of great concern. Overuse contaminates the food produced, and, in the long run, affects the consumer. The impact may be felt as far away as the Arctic.[6] Two French studies on pesticides have shown that half the fruits, vegetables, and cereals consumed in France contain pesticide residue. The second outlines the considerable risks these synthetic products cause to wild animals and to humans. Several pesticides are carcinogenic, affect the immune system, or slow children's growth.

Unfortunately, everywhere in the world, ministers of agriculture have, for a long time, given greater priority to concerted and highly productive agriculture than to consumers' health. This is due in part to the intense pressure applied by agrobusiness lobbyists. It's the reason why some people, myself included, favour the agricultural sector being placed under the jurisdiction of a larger ministry of Health and Consumption. Fortunately, events such as the mad cow disaster in England and dioxin-contaminated chicken in Belgium have made authorities take notice, and we are beginning, in France in particular, to apply the precautionary principle. But it must be extended to all those areas where there is potential risk to the public's health, and that has not yet happened.

For a number of reasons, including the exaggerated use of chemical products, we are witnessing a disturbing impoverishment of our soils, and also of the sea, which suffers from other problems.

FISHING

First, a personal anecdote. When I was a university student, I often spent my summer vacation in the Gaspé, in the Saint Lawrence River estuary. There is an odour that has stayed with me since that time: that of cod set out to dry on exposed surfaces in the sun. Approaching a village on foot, when the wind was blowing in the right direction, you became aware of it before you saw the first houses. Fishing was omnipresent in every village: nets put out to dry, boats re-tarred in dry dock, fish markets.

The fishermen sometimes let me go with them out to sea. We left at four in the morning and fished for several hours. One detail struck me, the significance of which I only understood later. Because of the possibility of inspections, we had to hide the small, undersized fish you could not legally catch. The reason was that, already for several years, a decrease in the number of cod had been observed. To fill their quotas, the fishermen caught smaller and smaller cod. They took females too young to have produced any eggs. The result: before long, there was nothing in the nets. Suddenly, a few years later, fishing was totally banned. Despite this action, the populations have not recovered.

I went back recently to that little village in the Gaspé. In a bar, a young man was humming a song called, "Plus jamais la mer," or "Never Again the Sea." It spoke of an out-of-work father's idleness, and of times past when, pipe in hand, the old cod fishermen took care to pass on their craft to their children, so they might carry it on. It was a sad and nostalgic song, and all the young people in the bar took up the refrain.

We are witnessing, overall, a widespread depletion of the fisheries. Maritime fishing has stagnated since 1990.[7] This is principally due to an increasing scarcity of fish. With all countries competing against each other, fishing boats were built that were more and more efficient and sophisticated, and caught more fish as rapidly as possible. They were equipped with nets several kilometres long, able to scrape the ocean floor. As a result, many species were fished quicker than they could reproduce. No one wanted to admit that the quantity of fish was finite.

Today, we know that the numbers have decreased alarmingly over the last ten years. More than 75% of the fishing grounds have reached their peak or are in decline. The most commercially popular fish have declined by 25%. In the North Sea, we have seen a collapse of mackerel stocks, with no recovery in sight (*Figure* 3.7). The salmon population is dropping dangerously. The skate has almost disappeared, thanks to dragnets. Other threatened species include haddock, hake, and cod, whose fishing is today prohibited (*Figure* 3.8).

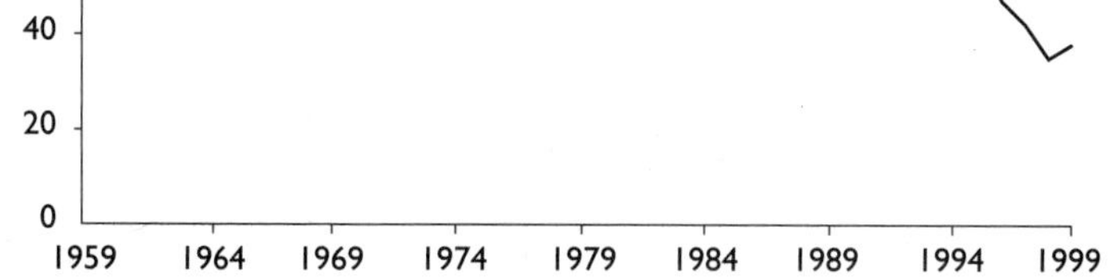

Figure 3.7. The quantity of mackerel fished since 1959.
SOURCE: IFREMER: FRENCH RESEARCH INSTITUTE FOR EXPLOITATION OF THE SEA.

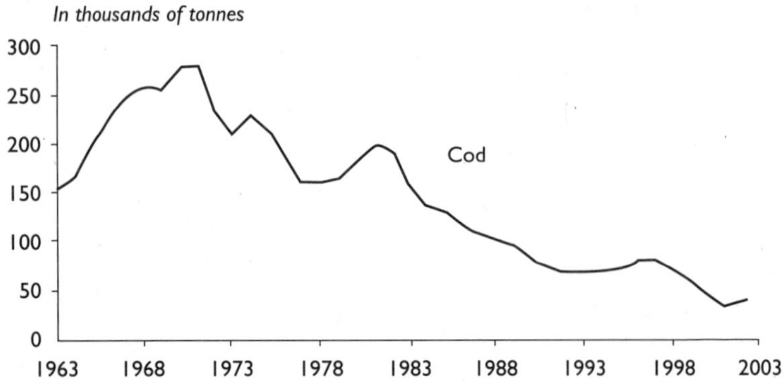

Figure 3.8. The population of adult female cod in the North Sea since 1963.

We are witnessing a chain reaction: the decrease in whiting has reduced the number of Steller sea lions in Alaska by 90%. The number of Japanese sardines has shrunk by 90% in twelve years.

Overfishing is the principal cause for the increasing scarcity of certain species. The decline in the number of fish is also due to the deterioration of the coastal zones: degassing of boats, oil exploitation, aquaculture. Freshwater fish are also threatened by various sorts of pollution and are particularly vulnerable because they cannot escape to other ecosystems when pollution has damaged their habitat.[8]

Might aquaculture be a solution? Not really, if we consider that these fish are being fed with substances that are themselves the product of harvests from the land.[9]

WATER

This brings us to the question of water. The world's available fresh water is unequally distributed. Some regions of the world have abundant reserves, while others are cruelly deprived of it. The Amazon Basin, for instance, contains 15% of the world's reserves and 0.3% of the population, while Asia only has 30% of the reserves, for 60% of the

Earth's population. That makes for conflict between neighbouring countries. Such conflicts may be observed in several places.[10] For instance, the Farakka Dam, which diverts the waters of the Ganges towards the Indian megalopolis of Calcutta, is responsible for tense relations between India and Bangladesh. Comparable conflicts exist between Turkey and Iraq, Ethiopia and Egypt, and between Israelis and Palestinians.

According to a study published by the International Programme for Technology and Research in Irrigation and Drainage (IPTRID),[11] competition for water resources will intensify in the Mediterranean basin over the next decades, and will significantly exacerbate the current water shortage. Of the twenty-one countries that have declared themselves short of water, twelve are concentrated in the Middle East, and many of them border the Mediterranean. "Despite the shortage of water, we observe a poor general use of resources," the report states. "In the Mediterranean basin, agriculture is considered the sector that could economize the greatest volume of water." With 80% of the total demand, Mediterranean agriculture is the greatest consumer of fresh water, but farmers do not use it wisely.

What makes things worse is water pollution caused by industrial and domestic waste. Marine ecosystems are vulnerable to pollution caused by a growing volume of used water and urban, industrial, and agricultural runoff, but also by fallout from atmospheric pollution.

In Brittany, pig farms produce liquid manure, a fertilizer rich in nitrate, in too great a quantity for agricultural lands. The result is massive pollution of groundwater. It becomes so polluted that some farmers have been forced to give their cows bottled water to drink.[12] The French audit office recently published a very harsh report bearing on the public water policies in Brittany. It analyzed seven programs put into practice in 1993 that were designed to halt the deterioration of the water supply in the region. Its conclusions brooked no contradiction: the state's record was "very mediocre, even disastrous." The 310 million Euros brought to bear on different measures "financed by taxpayers and consumers and that benefited almost exclusively the farmers, did not prevent a worsening of the pollution."

In Canada, agricultural activity is responsible for 80% of water pollution. Intensive agriculture, involving the use of an enormous quantity of chemical products, has generated significant pollution levels, especially in the groundwater. Most of the fresh water that we drink or use in agriculture and industry does not come from the surface, but from the underground water table. Specific geological formations (sand, gravel, rock) have held back rain water or melted ice water for very long periods of time. As a result, 97% of the liquid fresh water on the planet is stored in these water tables.

Given the many kinds of pollution that have affected our waterways and lakes, we are relying increasingly on these reserves of underground water. But they are being polluted more and more by chemical products used in industry and now, above all, in agriculture. Several agricultural pesticides kill wild animals directly, or accumulate in the food chain, exposing those consumers at the end of the chain, including humans, to toxic substances.

This pollution, increasingly widespread, exacerbates a serious problem where our reserves of fresh water are concerned. It seems that we have suddenly realized that these resources are finite, and that we are about to face shortages.

In the course of the twentieth century, water consumption multiplied by a factor of seven, and the population by three (*Figure* 3.9). Agriculture requires more and more. Today, it consumes 70% of fresh water, compared with 20% for industry and 10% for domestic use. The levels of groundwater are falling rapidly. In the north of China, levels are going down 1.5 metres per year. In India, the rate of water extraction is twice as great as the rate at which the water table replenishes itself. Result: not only is the groundwater increasingly polluted, but in some areas, such as in California, it is beginning to disappear.

The Aral Sea in Central Asia was once the fourth largest lake on

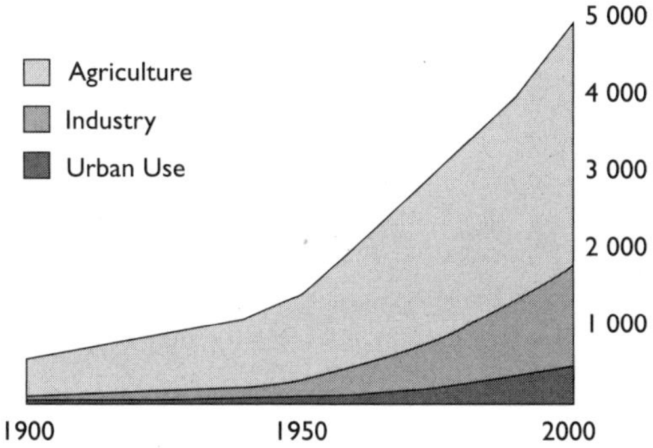

Canada	98.5 m³ per person
Brazil	42.96
Australia	19.0
Hungary	11.9
Mexico	3.8
France	3.4
China	2.3
India	2.2
Egypt	0.9
Israel	0.4

Figure 3.9. Increase in water consumption for different uses (urban, industrial, agricul-tural) since 1900, in cubic kilometres, on a global scale. On the right, the available water reserves (in cubic metres per person) in different countries.

SOURCE: *Times*, NOVEMBER 1997.

the planet. Now it is almost dried up. It has lost four-fifths of its surface.[13] The two rivers that fed it, the Amu Darya and the Syr Darya, were diverted to irrigate cotton fields. The result was an ecological disaster: the desertification of its ancient surface, and radical salinization of the neighbouring water tables. What is more, the intensive farming brought contamination by pesticides. An increase in hepatitis, respiratory illnesses, and anemia has been observed.

We mustn't delude ourselves: we are approaching a depletion of drinkable water. Some foresee that as early as 2025, two-thirds of the world's population will be subject to water shortages.

THE "CLEANING UP" OF SWAMPS

To this shortage of drinking water we can also add the disappearance, especially in North America, of most wetlands — victims of commercial exploitation, transformation into agricultural lands, or adaptation to other uses. The Earth has lost 50% of its marshlands since 1900.[14] These are regions where flooding is frequent and where the water does not exceed a depth of six metres. Such marshlands are home to many animal and plant communities, and are of crucial importance to the survival of certain threatened species, including migratory birds. What is more, they decontaminate rivers and streams of their many toxins and the excess nitrate and phosphorus caused by fertilization. They regulate the flow of water, replenish groundwater, and prevent flooding in other regions. And they are very difficult to restore.

The depletion of energy sources, the depletion of the soil and wetlands, the depletion of water: mankind has pillaged and drained the entire planet in the course of a few decades.

THE MASSACRE OF THE FORESTS

We must add to this list of depleted resources and natural environments the problem of the forests. An astronaut told me of the sad spectacle, viewed from space, of Brazilian, African, and Indonesian territories sending forth huge plumes of smoke. During the twentieth century, we destroyed half the world's forest land.

This deforestation is continuing, amid general indifference, at the rate of two football fields per second.[15] About 150 corporations dominate the world market for forest products. Most refuse to exploit varieties of wood that are not threatened, as they are less profitable. They are only interested in varieties that grow in primary forests. Today, according to the World Resource Institute, 80% of these have disappeared from the surface of the globe.

These primary forests have not been previously altered by human activity. They represent an extraordinary biological richness. The largest are to be found in the Amazon, in the Congo basin in Africa, and in Southeast Asia.

The Amazon forest is the greatest; but since 1950, 15% of its immense surface area has been destroyed.[16] The international community is trying today to preserve what is left, and to bring back those lands damaged by burning.

The Indonesian forests are among the most biologically rich on the planet. The forest of Tesso Nilo, in particular, is in imminent danger of extinction — which in its wake would cause the disappearance of elephants, tigers, tapirs, monkeys, and hundreds of very rare plants. Plans to save it have been sabotaged by illegal cutting and corruption.[17] Mexico is the fourth most important global region in the diversity of forest species. But it is estimated that this country has already lost 95% of its tropical rainforests. Mexico's deforestation has resulted from a number of underlying factors, including population growth, agricultural restructuring, discriminatory land use policies, and government programs for colonization.

Many other forests around the world are threatened, such as Marmora, a magnificent forest of cork oaks in Morocco, which was once one of the greatest and most magnificent forests in North Africa. Located on the threshold of Rabat, today it's in danger of disappearing, a casualty of human activity.

THE FUTURE

Given this alarming state of affairs, what are our hopes for the future? How do we remedy the depletion of resources and natural habitats? We are faced with a paradoxical situation. On the one hand, we must do everything possible to facilitate a significant expansion in agriculture and an increase in food production, which is still possible. On the other hand, this expansion will doubtlessly result in more deforestation, the loss of species, soil erosion, and pollution by pesticides and fertilizer, which must absolutely be halted.

We must therefore increase the productivity of cultivated land without polluting. UN experts remain relatively optimistic: this requirement will stimulate agricultural innovation. Land being used less constructively will become agricultural. There is also great unrealized potential in the use of agricultural residue: cornstalks, and rice and wheat straw can be used to feed animals. More importantly, we can eliminate the intensive use of nitrates by organizing a better rotation of crops, as is already done in a number of Asian countries. We can also do without insecticides, or find natural alternatives to them. In 1986 in Indonesia, the government banned fifty-seven pesticides, and significantly reduced their application. Pesticide use went down by 60%, and rice harvests increased by 25%.

Personally, I favour the development of organic agriculture. Even if in France it represents only a small percentage of overall agricultural production, many growers are converting to this form of cultivation, which better respects the soil, and uses no chemical products.[18]

As for fishing, there is no other solution than to limit it, and to create, as has been done for the last twenty-five years, protected zones near the coasts so that marine populations may recover. But these zones must be enlarged. Today, they represent only a small fraction of the ocean's surface.

Regulations must have teeth. There is a striking gap between the seriousness and the urgency of these problems and the very weak measures taken against polluters and those who contravene measures designed to protect the seas and the forests. International reports and those prepared by the French audit office consistently identify abuses and evasions of all sorts, but nothing seems to change. How to remedy the situation? Harsher punishment and better supervision? Improved education and sensitization for citizens and the most important players involved: farmers and fishermen?

Tensions have developed in many areas of the world between producers and environmentalists. In Newfoundland, for example, they have come to blows over the annual seal hunt on numerous occasions. There is only one way to resolve these conflicts, which only lead to paralysis, and that is to invite the representatives of both parties to the same table, first to take stock of the situation in an objective way, and then to make common cause in advocating reform.

Recently, I was presented with just such a situation on the Madeleine

Islands in the Gulf of Saint Lawrence. The lobster fishermen, aware of the disarray in the cod fishery, decided among themselves to reduce the size of their lobster pots and to increase the size of the mesh in their nets in order to avoid capturing young lobster. The result: the fishing is going ahead at a pace adapted to reproduction.

The education of those concerned, and summit meetings that will establish a common front to steer away from disaster represent, I believe, the best approach for the future.

Nonetheless, despite a real awakening on the part of public opinion in the West, and some useful measures to which we will return, the situation continues to worsen.[19]

GMOS

We must address the issue of genetically modified organisms (GMOs), especially considering that the aggressive actions taken against them have received widespread media attention, and people are wondering what to think.

Let us first make clear that a genetically modified organism is an organism to which one has added or from which one has subtracted a function. Result: it is endowed with new possibilities that modify its behaviour, making it, for example, more resistant to the diseases that afflict its species.

GMOs raise a lot of difficult questions, and it would be best to treat the subject on a case by case basis. Opinions are divided. The most serious problem according to experts is the scattering of GMO seeds beyond the prescribed territory, and the contamination of non-GMO species with a combination of genetic variations and resistances both unforeseen and undesirable in wild plants.[20]

It is not the farmers of Africa or Asia, nor even Western farmers, who asked for GMOs. It's understandable that representatives of the agricultural community are concerned and protest — all the more in that they risk becoming dependent on biogenetic firms. There is a widespread feeling that these firms are applying pressure in order to impose, as rapidly as possible, potentially profitable innovations, showing no concern for the fact that their monopoly on seeds will lead to the disappearance of small farmers, and that their blunders could spin out of control. It's a plunge into the unknown, and it's not hard to imagine, with anxiety already running high, a calamitous scenario.

On the question of health, it seems to me that it is still too soon to assert with confidence that there is no risk. For example, the UN's spokesperson on food rights, Jean Ziegler, came out with a negative opinion, stating that the GMOs "could constitute a medium- or long-term danger for the human organism and public health." The debate between experts is far from over, and independent sources such as the CRII-Gen, an independent research and information committee on genetic engineering, has denounced the position of the Academies. The Academies often ground their arguments not so much in science and medicine, but in economics, which is not their field, without taking into account the environmental consequences of GMOs. Without being radically hostile to GMOs, I fear that overly strong economic pressures may stifle the sort of complex debate that must take place before a moratorium is lifted.

4

A SOILED PLANET

The Augean Stables

FROM EARLIER CHAPTERS, IT SEEMS clear that not only does man pillage the Earth and deplete its resources, he seriously pollutes it. What sort of planet are we going to leave to our descendants, and above all, what can we do about the problem?

Among the twelve labours imposed on Hercules by Eurystheus, king of Tiryns, was the cleansing of the Augean stables. It was considered a superhuman task. This myth seems appropriate for our time.

The soiling of the planet is a stark reality to us at present, as we behold beaches covered in viscous oil and gluey birds, the result of an endless series of shipwrecks involving rusted out boats.

Like the beach cleaners with their shovels, we are faced, on a planetary scale, with a gigantic task. All through the twentieth century, mankind accumulated a quantity of garbage much more dangerous than what had been generated in previous millennia. To all the pollution already described — household, industrial, agricultural — we may add the stocks of terribly destructive weapons that have been building up, for the most part, since the First World War. We usually think of weapons as an active threat, but rarely as a source of pollution.

ANTI-PERSONNEL MINES

Stockpiles of arms are a significant source of pollution and an enormous potential danger, even when there is no longer any intention to put them to use. Take the example of anti-personnel mines. The first mines, which were really buried bombs, were used by England in the fifteenth century during the Battle of Agincourt, and then more systematically in the nineteenth century during the American Civil War. During World War II, more than three hundred million anti-tank mines were deployed by the warring parties. But these mines had the disadvantage of being easily transportable and reusable by the enemy. To prevent this, small anti-personnel mines were manufactured and placed around the anti-tank mines. Subsequently, their military purpose changed, and they were used to target civilian populations. Since they were well camouflaged and remained active for more than seventy-five years, they continued to mutilate and kill civilians, even in times of peace. It has been calculated that around the globe, anti-personnel mines claim a victim every twenty minutes. A hundred and ten million have been deployed in seventy-five countries.[1]

The principal mine fields are found in Africa, the most thickly mined continent in the world, with nearly fifty million mines. There are some two and a half million in Zimbabwe, and, after twenty years of civil war, fifteen million buried around villages in Angola, where in a population of just thirteen million inhabitants, there are sixty-five thousand amputees.

In the Middle East, Iraqi Kurdistan and Iran are mined, as are, farther east, Afghanistan and Kashmir. Southeast Asia, Vietnam, Thailand, and Cambodia are the most affected. Cambodia was mined during three successive conflicts: the war against the United States, the takeover by the Khmer Rouge, and the conflicts between Cambodian factions and the pro-Vietnamese regime. The result is that for a population of ten million inhabitants, there are nearly five million mines, or one mine for every two people.

Some European countries are also mined, principally the former Yugoslavia, but also, in lesser measure, Germany and Belgium, where mines that date from the First World War are still being discovered.

Beyond the dramatic consequences for human beings, these mines constitute an economic and environmental disaster. When the containers break down, highly toxic substances leak into the soil, polluting the countryside over large areas.

In Cambodia, for example, they have reduced the arable land north of Tonle Sap Lake and in the Mekong Delta. The result is an increase in malnutrition, a rural exodus towards Phnom Penh and Battambang, and urban overpopulation. In this same country, the mines also inhibit commerce, making roads, such as those between Battambang and Pursat or Pailin, impassable.

Some countries are actively demining the affected areas, but the costs are prohibitive. A small anti-personnel mine costs about $3 to make, but between $300 and $1,000 to find, extract, and destroy. As for the artificial prostheses needed for the tens of thousands of survivors, they cost between $100 and $3,000 and must be replaced every five years for an adult and every six months for a child.

The paradox is that these mines continue to be purchased and set. Fifty or so countries continue to manufacture them, including Russia, the United States, and many developing countries, despite the fact that the production and sales of these weapons have been strictly prohibited by international treaties. The end of the Cold War and stock-taking by non-governmental organizations (NGOs) has led certain states to decree a moratorium on their production and export. The Ottawa Treaty, which outlawed the sale of anti-personnel mines, was signed by 120 countries in December 1997. The problem arises from those countries that did not sign the treaty, such as Afghanistan, Cambodia, Vietnam, Mozambique, and so on. To that, we must also add illegal trafficking on the part of those countries that did sign.

Since we have embarked on a rather sinister tour of the territory, let us look at the stockpiles of weapons of mass destruction assembled during the twentieth century.

THE CHEMICAL ARSENAL

If we take these weapons in order of their appearance, we must talk first about chemical weapons. The synthesis of mustard gas goes back to the middle of the nineteenth century. The Germans used it at Ypres, in Belgium, during the First World War, but not during World War II, even though the Allies found vast quantities stored in German factories. They too, in fact, had large amounts in their possession.

Shortly after the Second World War, three other toxic gases were synthesized: tabun, sarin, and soman. Iraq used tabun during the war against Iran and against the Kurdish population, and we remember the use of sarin by the Aum Shinrikyo sect in the Tokyo subway, which took several lives in March 1995.

In 1983, an international agreement was signed, declaring that any country that used nerve gas would be severely punished. Only the United States, Russia, Iraq, and India admitted to having manufactured it. The Americans committed themselves to destroying 30,000 tonnes, and Russia, 40,000 tonnes. Iraq claimed to have destroyed its reserves, and India characterized its own use as "purely defensive." Other countries are suspected of possessing it, including North Korea, Egypt, Israel, Syria, Libya, China, Iran, South Africa, and France.[2]

After the Second World War, we had to dispose of these toxic gases quickly: the Nazis left behind 300,000 tonnes of nerve gas. The allies loaded the German stockpile onto boats, and sunk the boats in the vicinity of Norway. In 1967, the United States did the same thing with nerve gas rockets off the coast of New Jersey. Despite advice to the contrary, these chemical weapons were most often dumped into shallow water, and in fishing grounds. Bombs of mustard gas have been found in nets on German and Polish beaches. The shallow Baltic Sea (170 metres) was widely used as a dumping ground by the British, the Americans, and the Russians. Today, international conventions do not force countries to destroy the weapons, and dumping is prohibited. Despite everything, it continues to be practised in secret.

THE BACTERIOLOGICAL ARSENAL

After chemical weapons, we have to talk about bacteriological weapons, which use germs. According to the experts, they are much more dangerous than chemical weapons. They have returned to the limelight following the events of September 11, 2001, and the delivery of mail containing anthrax.

The oldest example of this type of weapon is the dead rat that was thrown into enemies' wells during the Middle Ages. The idea of concentrating the bacteria of diseases like the plague or cholera in order to infect whole populations arose in the twentieth century. Unlike chemical weapons, bacteriological weapons have been little used in recent conflicts, except during the Japanese attacks in China, and perhaps other Asian countries, before and during the Second World War. Bacteriological weapons were stockpiled during both world wars.

The United States did not terminate their offensive program until

1969, and Russia is suspected of maintaining its program, begun during the Soviet era.

Many different bacteria have been tried. The Japanese used the plague bacillus against the Chinese in Manchuria. But it caused damage on both sides. Today, our mastery of these lethal technologies is much more sophisticated. A very small quantity of a product will kill many people. For example, a single gram of botulinus toxin could kill a million people.

These bacteria are intended as offensive weapons. I saw a television interview with a Russian engineer who, for twenty-five years, was the director of a biological weapons complex divided into eight different centres near Moscow, and employing more than twenty thousand people. Small, dry, impassive, he spoke of the enormous difficulties his laboratories faced in perfecting weapons that could conserve, store, transport, and vaporize tonnes of organisms, while preserving their infectious capabilities. The buzz word for this process is "weaponize." What was most striking was his obvious absence of feeling when discussing the nature of his enterprise and the possible consequences of his actions.

Despite the international convention that outlaws such weapons coming into force in 1975, the US Congressional Office of Technology Assessment drew up, in 1993, a list of eight countries known to have an undeclared program for manufacturing offensive biological weapons.[3] They are Iran, Iraq, Israel, Libya, Syria, China, North Korea, and Taiwan. Six other countries suspected of having comparable programs were also named: Egypt, Vietnam, Laos, Cuba, Bulgaria, and India. Romania and South Africa have also been accused of following suit.

In 1992, Boris Yeltsin admitted that, in the past, the Soviets had undertaken an ambitious program of biological weaponry. There were even serious accidents that were, of course, kept secret. In 1992, Yeltsin wanted to dismantle these laboratories and to conform to the Biological Weapons Convention (BWC), which was ratified two decades earlier but largely ignored.

The United States only ended its own offensive program in 1969. Today, it refuses to subject itself to supervision by the Biological Weapons Convention on the grounds that it must protect its laboratories and pharmaceutical companies from industrial espionage.[4] After the incident with the anthrax being sent through the postal system, the US Army had to admit that it continued to manufacture it at its Dugway Proving Ground installations in Utah.

It would appear that the bacteriological threat has replaced the nuclear threat in people's minds. And in fact, I believe that biological weapons represent a much more serious threat to the future than nuclear weapons. They can be acquired and manipulated more easily by rogue states or terrorist groups, which makes them all the more frightening.

THE NUCLEAR ARSENAL

The end of the Cold War had the happy consequence of significantly reducing the number of nuclear warheads. After climbing to almost a hundred thousand, their number today is somewhat more than twenty thousand,[5] and new reductions are expected[6] (*Figure 4.1*).

As for France, it is currently dismantling its arsenal on the Albion Plateau and is converting the facility into research laboratories. Russia still produces nuclear weapons, but its means are very restricted. In Russia, the real danger today is the exportation of its radioactive material, its technology, and its engineers to rogue states or terrorist groups.[7] The United States stopped producing nuclear weapons in 1990, but still researches new models through simulation.

There is a concerted effort underway today to adapt these radioactive substances for the civilian nuclear industry. Great quantities of uranium and plutonium are stockpiled in thousands of nuclear warheads. They are also found in ships' reactors and in atomic submarines.

The most dramatic case is that of hundreds of ships abandoned by the Soviets at the end of the Cold War in the Barents Sea near Norway with no surveillance. They represent 24,000 tonnes of nuclear fuel subject to corrosion, of which radioactive discharge has already been detected in the water. Several countries, including Norway in particular, recently decided to help Russia clean up this site.[8]

The production centres for atomic weapons have become radioactive dumps that will cost considerable sums to clean up. At Hanford in the United States,[9] birthplace of the first atomic bombs, ten thousand people on a 1,500 square kilometre site will work over a period of fifty years to do away with 1,400 tonnes of radioactive discharge and 2,100 tonnes of nuclear fuel (including 7 tonnes of plutonium). The total cost of the operation is estimated at more than fifty billion American dollars.

Vast regions of the former USSR have become uninhabitable. Chelyabinsk, one of the centres of military production specializing in the manufacture of nuclear weapons, is one example.[10] Multiple accidents poisoned a vast sector of the province. At the beginning of the 1950s, twenty-two villages were evacuated. A 1957 accident twice as serious as Chernobyl was kept secret for a long time, and necessitated the evacuation of 10,700 people.

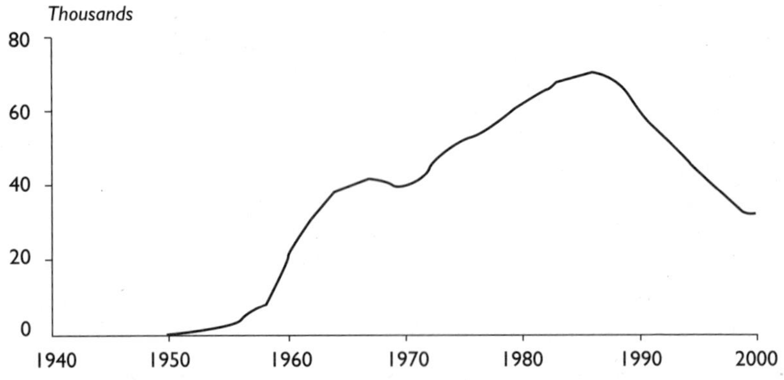

Figure 4.1. The number of nuclear warheads on the planet. The decrease begun in the 1980s continues today.

SOURCE: *Vital Signs*, 2001, P. 87.

CHEMICAL INDUSTRIAL WASTE

Following this survey of fear-inspiring military arsenals, we must now consider the waste produced and built up by civilian industry, agriculture, and domestic activities. First, the waste generated by the civilian nuclear industry, a subject we dealt with in some detail in the chapter on energy.

Between the wars, the chemical industry made great advances, and numerous substances destined for industry or agriculture were produced in the laboratory. After the Second World War, chemistry made inroads into our lives through, for example, the pesticides we used in agriculture, but also all the products used in paint, varnish, cleaning products, detergents, etc. Today, more than a hundred thousand different chemical products are on sale around the world, and nearly a thousand new products appear on the market each year.[11]

It took many years before the toxicity of certain products was recognized. Thus DDT (see Chapter 2), commercialized in 1938 and promoted as a miracle insecticide, was finally banned in 1972. In the meantime, more than three million tonnes of this dangerous product were released into the environment. In 1980, the World Health Organization (WHO) declared that pesticides caused almost twenty thousand deaths and nearly three million poisonings of one sort or another each year, especially in poor countries where no precautions were taken. The same goes for polychlorobiphenyls (PCBs), which were introduced in 1929, and can be found in many popular products, such as paints, varnishes, etc. It became clear that this substance infiltrated the land and sea environments and affected the immune systems and reproductive organs of living organisms. This is the most plausible explanation for the decimation of seals, dolphins, and porpoises since the middle of the 1980s. These marine mammals concentrate pesticides in their flesh for years, and eventually succumb to minor infections due to the radical weakening of their immune systems.

TOXIC RISKS

Might these diseases of the immune system and reproductive organs affect human beings, who find themselves at the end of the food chain, and are endowed with a long lifespan that could favour the accumulation of a number of chemical substances? It's still difficult to have a clear idea of how the human species has been affected by PCBs. In industrialized countries we see a constant increase in breast cancer and cancer of the reproductive organs, which could have a direct connection with this kind of poisoning. In 1950, one American woman out of twenty developed breast cancer, compared with one out of eight today. We also observe an increase in estrogen due to the fact that PCBs trigger hormonal irregularities. Due to this increase, what has been widely seen in the animal world (instances of sterility and male malformation) has started to appear in men. Human males have already lost almost half of their spermatozoids (*Figure 4.2*).

Grave problems have also been associated with the domestic use of toxic substances, such as formaldehyde used in the polishing of

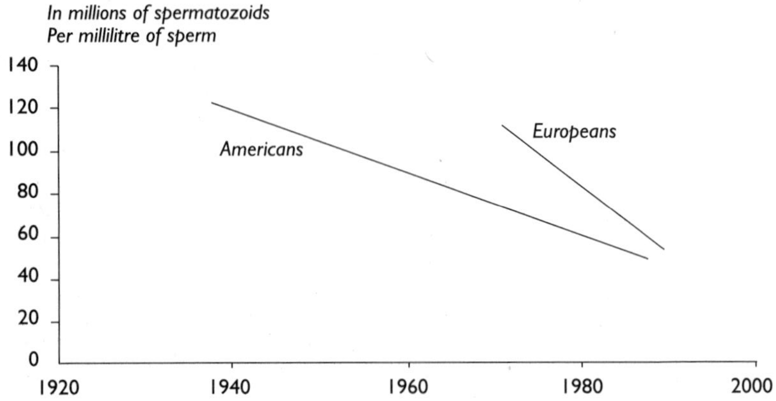

Figure 4.2. Decrease in the concentration of spermatozoids in the sperm of Americans and Europeans since 1938.

furniture, in glues, varnishes, cleaning sprays, etc. These cause allergies, asthma, and are probably carcinogenic. The air in our houses is polluted. One solution is regular ventilation. Open your windows.[12]

There is also the treatment of wood with copper arsenate, which gives it such a pretty green tint. Invented in India in 1933, the product protects the wood against insects and mould. Children play on the treated surfaces and put their fingers in their mouths, causing serious health problems.

POLLUTION FROM MINING AND BLACK TIDES

We have already mentioned the black pollution caused by the shipwrecks of great oil tankers (*Amoco Cadiz, Erika, Prestige*, etc.) and the sticky masses that wash up on the coasts, paralyzing fisheries and killing tens of thousands of birds.

To that we must add the polluting substances[13] used in the extraction of minerals and oil. Every mining region, active or abandoned, retains its dose of toxic substances for a long time, such as mercury, that make their way into the environment and often destroy the flora and fauna over great distances.

PLASTIC WASTE

But we must also talk about plastic, invented shortly after the First World War. It would be hard to tally all the advantages and services this material provides.[14] But its very qualities also constitute its greatest drawback: it takes decades, if not centuries, for it to break down. Its waste just stays there, on beaches, beside waterways, and in the desert around oases, where the landscape is utterly marred by plastic bags whipped by the wind. During a trek of several days in the Tunisian Sahara, our first sign of an oasis was a flight of coloured plastic bags. Noah's dove had undergone a sad metamorphosis.

We now know that sea-borne plastic debris, the quantity of which is a hundred times greater than in 1990, carries numerous organisms that, having reached distant islands or mainland shores, represent a serious threat to the local fauna and flora.[15]

The list of civilian waste includes many other undesirable substances. And the list is long. According to the FAO, 500,000 tonnes of out of date pesticide, unused or banned, is stockpiled in rural areas, near fields and wells. Just like the 600,000 tonnes of animal meal that could not be used after the "mad cow" episode. We don't know how to get rid of it all without spending colossal sums.

Even if we don't have irrefutable proof, the public must at least be warned. The problem is that, for reasons of economic profitability, we do not take the time to properly test new substances put on the market. It often takes many years to determine whether a product is toxic. All products that are undeniably toxic are prohibited, but they continue to poison us for a long time, most often through the food chain. Some products, like DDT, were banned thirty years ago, but we'll have to wait nearly a century before they disappear from contaminated areas. Not to mention the fact that they are still used secretly in some developing countries. We've already seen this problem in the case of nitrate pollution of water tables. We don't know how long it would take for them to become pure once more, even if we were to halt all new pollution immediately.

CHEMICAL EXPLOSIONS

The last point I want to make concerns the risk of chemical explosions. In 1976, the Seveso tragedy in northern Italy alerted experts to the dangers associated with the functioning of chemical factories. In 1982, a "Seveso" list was drawn up of dangerous sites. But the explosion of the AZF factory in Toulouse, even if the causes remain unknown, show that the problem is still very much with us and can become worse as installations age and nearby populations increase.

We could also cite the Bhopal disaster in India, the night of December 2 to 3, 1984, which caused more than two thousand deaths on the spot and left sixty thousand seriously injured, not to mention the tens of thousands of deformed children born after the tragedy. These dramatic accidents will continue unless we can close down all the factories that present a danger.

And there are other problems. In France, for example — but these proportions per inhabitant are about the same everywhere — every year individuals produce about 20 million tonnes of waste, industries 150 million, and agriculture, including the agro-industries, 400 million. It is this last sector that is the biggest producer of waste, but also the most responsible for pollution of the soil and water, as we have already noted.

For the planet as a whole, we calculate about a billion tonnes of urban waste alone, most often discharged in open air dumps, as in Peking, which contains four thousand tonnes. To avoid that, we must work either upstream, eliminating certain non-degradable or toxic materials, or downstream, by burning the wastes and recovering the heat, as is done in the Paris region.

As for the wastes produced by industry and agriculture, they present so many problems and are still so frequently discharged into the environment that they will be polluting for a long time.

THE POLLUTION OF SPACE

We'll soon have to live in space if we want to find an unpolluted environment. But not too close to the Earth because, besides atmospheric pollution, the planet is surrounded by about ten thousand pieces of debris associated with various experiments in space and the launching of satellites.[16] This debris circles the Earth, fencing it in with a ring of flying objects that poses a danger to scientific satellites and to the international space station. It is also responsible for light pollution. In breaking up, it creates a nebulous layer, like a fog, that absorbs and relays sunlight, creating a problem for astronomical observation. Although those objects orbiting at low altitude eventually fall back into the atmosphere and disintegrate, above 1000 kilometres they are there forever.

LIGHT POLLUTION IN OUR SKIES

One of the biggest casualties of industrialization on a global scale is the contact we human beings have with the stars. Today, the stars, the planets, the Milky Way, that for so long were nighttime companions to human beings, are unknown to a large part of the population. Urban street lighting, the lighting along roads, essential of course but often excessive, cuts us off from the deep emotion we all feel on a dark night when the sky is filled with stars. Today, there is a growing movement, initiated by amateur astronomers, demanding a reduction in this lighting to restore to people the possibility of gazing at the stars.[17]

THE DAUNTING TASK ...

It took less than a day for Hercules to clean up the Augean stables. Even if mankind were to halt all pollution immediately, which is not foreseeable, it would take centuries to eliminate the toxic waste that taints the air, earth, and waters on our beautiful planet.

Appendix

4.1. THE HISTORY AND STATUS OF NUCLEAR ARMAMENTS

Let us briefly review the history of nuclear weapons. Leo Szilard, the Hungarian-American physicist, was the first to discover, in 1939, the theoretical possibility of making an atomic bomb. In 1941, he launched the Manhattan Project, which culminated in 1945 with the first experimental explosion at Alamogordo, New Mexico. One year later, two Japanese cities, Hiroshima and Nagasaki, were obliterated, and over two hundred thousand people died. Following that event, the arms race between the Americans and the Russians escalated relentlessly. In 1954, the Americans developed two deuterium and lithium hydrogen bombs of 15 and 11 megatonnes, 750 and 500 times stronger, respectively, than the Hiroshima bomb. On October 30, 1961, the USSR exploded a 58 megatonne bomb, three thousand times more powerful than Hiroshima. At the height of the Cold War, from the end of 1961 to the end of 1962, the Americans and Soviets triggered 170 nuclear explosions, 110 in the atmosphere. The radioactivity in the air increased substantially. Following the Cuban missile crisis, the Partial Test Ban Treaty (PTBT) was signed on August 5, 1963. It prohibited nuclear explosions in the atmosphere, in space, and underwater. The Threshold Test Ban Treaty (TTBT), signed in 1974, limited underground explosions to 150 kilotonnes. The moratorium decreed by the USSR during the years 1985 and 1986 had no impact. On the contrary, the Pentagon proceeded during that time period with twenty-three tests.

With the fall of the Berlin Wall and the end of the Cold War, the number of tests decreased. By 1992, they were down to fewer than ten per year. In 1996, the General Assembly of the United Nations adopted the text of the Comprehensive Test Ban Treaty (CTBT) by 158 votes to three, with five abstentions. Given the refusal of India, the CTBT was more or less preserved in the form of an adopted resolution. By 1998, 150 governments had signed it, but only twenty countries had ratified it. The adopted resolution restricted itself to demanding a halt to all nuclear tests, which meant that the Non-Proliferation Treaty, updated in 1995, was not reduced to nothing. In 2002, the treaty entirely prohibiting nuclear tests had still not been put into force. Of the forty-four countries with nuclear reactors whose ratification is required for the agreement to be put into effect, only thirty-one have deposited their instruments of ratification. Another source of tension is the American Anti-missile Shield project, which is a threat to the limitation and reduction of strategic offensive weapons.

5

THE ANIMALS, OUR BROTHERS

I am the brother in God of all that lives, as much of the giraffe and the crocodile as of man, and I am the fellow citizen of all that inhabit the Grand Hotel of the Universe.

GUSTAVE FLAUBERT

BIODIVERSITY IN CRISIS

Research in agronomy, pharmacology, and more generally in many industry fields, often points out the losses that could result from the disappearance of certain living species. To deal adequately with this question, it seems essential to me that, from the very start, we distance ourselves from our anthropocentric view of nature.

Living beings exist in their own right and do not have to justify their existence. The expressions "harmful species" and "weeds" only reflect an age-old prejudice going back to Genesis[1] to the effect that plants and animals are there to serve us or to give us pleasure, and that we have discretionary rights over them. In fact, we are only one species among others, and, given the disappearances for which we are responsible, we are the ones who deserve to be characterized as a species harmful to nature's harmony and the preservation of biodiversity.

Every extinction is an irreparable loss, a heart-wrenching disaster. This is the first and most important justification for preserving diversity. All species that exist have, de facto, the right to exist, and human beings have a duty to protect them and not to bring about their extermination.

Another reason to preserve nature's biodiversity is its vast palette of forms and colours. Every plant, every animal is a marvel, an incarnation of life's prodigious inventiveness and creativity as it has unfolded over hundreds of millions of years, and of which we are the product. The spectacle of plant life burgeoning in the spring, the return of migratory birds, these are sights cruelly lacking to modern man, largely restricted to a concrete urban environment. Rejoicing in nature's beauty is crucial to our psychic well-being.

Having made this clear, we can go on to deal with the economic and medical possibilities sacrificed to the impoverishment of biodiversity.[2] Pharmacology has greatly benefited from the traditional medicinal lore of different cultures. In the vast assemblage of plants not yet identified or poorly known, there is doubtlessly an abundance of new cures that will never heal anyone if we allow them to disappear.

EXTINCTIONS

One might argue that the extinction of living organisms has occurred all through the Earth's history. Life is in continual flux. Species die off, while others, better adapted, emerge. Why, today, should we refuse to accept the disappearance of certain species? Isn't that the law of nature itself?

It's true that the number of species has changed significantly throughout the Earth's history. The evolutionary process at work over billions of years has continually brought forth new species, while others disappeared. With the passing of time, between cataclysmic geological periods — meteorite showers, volcanism on a global scale, etc. — various disturbances, caused, for example, by climatic change, brought in their wake the elimination of certain species. But these losses were compensated for by the appearance of new species, better adapted to their environment.

With the development of agriculture and animal husbandry about ten thousand years ago, man became responsible for many disappearances. The industrial age radically accelerated the rate of extinction. According to a 2007 report by the IUCN (International Union for Conservation of Nature), one-fourth of mammals, one-eighth of birds, one-third of amphibians, and 70% of plants are threatened by extinction.

There are an estimated ten million species alive today on Earth, not counting viruses and bacteria. But this number is only an approximation.[3] Only 1.4 million species have been identified and named.[4] They include about 750,000 insects (of which 20,000 are butterflies), 250,000 plants, and 42,000 vertebrates.

To determine the fraction that has disappeared,[5] we use what is called "the Olaf Arrhenius and Edward O. Wilson principle" pertaining to the destruction of habitats. According to this principle, which has been widely authenticated in the field, it is estimated that when 50% of a given territory — an island, for example — has been destroyed, 90% of the native species have been exterminated. We should add that species are not interchangeable. The existence of each one — the product of billions of years of evolution — plays a role in the functioning of the ecosystem. From this point of view, the number of estimated extinctions is a gross understatement of the extent of the damage.

The causes for this exponential growth in the rate of extinction are many,[6] but they may all be traced back to one fundamental source: man's impact on nature. They include the destruction of natural environments and habitats, hunting, overfishing, poaching, pesticides, pollution, the greenhouse effect, the destruction of the ozone layer, and so on.

Many species whose numbers are shrinking or that are nearing extinction are utterly unknown to the general public. First, a personal experience. Twenty-five years ago, in our garden at Malicorne, I planted a *buddleia*, still called a butterfly tree. On hot summer days, I could count dozens of different varieties fluttering around the fragrant corollas. In recent years the population has greatly diminished. I've observed the same phenomenon with the swallows that made their nests in our old barns and the frogs that croaked in the pond. We don't see them anymore, or if we do, they are far fewer.[7]

A commission established by the Convention on International Trade in Endangered Species of Wild Fauna and Flora (CITES) is responsible for keeping track of endangered species and regulating trade involving them.[8]

Among large mammals, the rhinoceros is the most threatened in the short term. There were 70,000 in 1960, and only a few in 2008. Although protected, it is still poached for its horn. Elephants are rapidly disappearing since the international ivory trade resumed in 1997. Thirty years ago, there were two million. In 2007, there were only a few hundred thousand. As for the great cats, they are in peril because of the fragmentation of their habitat.[9]

Because of the warming of the polar regions, polar bears run the risk of being deprived of the conditions they need to survive.[10] The last ibex of the Pyrenees expired some years ago.

The territory of the Bonobo, the variety of chimpanzee closest to humans, bordered on the north by the Congo River and on the south by the Kasai River, is no more than 200,000 square kilometres. Its population has decreased from 100,000 in 1980 to a few thousand today. If deforestation and poaching continue, the species will soon disappear, as the female only gives birth to one child every five or six years.[11]

The situation is no more promising for sea mammals. Whales are in a difficult situation, especially the blue whale, of which there are only a few thousand specimens, while there were an estimated 200,000 or more in 1920. Even if their commercial fishing has been outlawed since 1986, several countries, such as Japan, Norway, and Iceland, contravene the law on the pretext of scientific research.[12]

We must also mention the extremely harmful effect of military sonar on these mammals. In March 2000, for example, fourteen whales were found stranded in the Bahamas, victims of brain hemorrhages inflicted by powerful sound waves. The U.S. Navy assumed responsibility.

The belugas in the Saint Lawrence River in Canada have the highest cancer rate (27%) of any mammal, and are also in the process of disappearing. Industrial pollution is presumed responsible for this disaster. Their population has shrunk from 5,000 at the beginning of the twentieth century to a few hundred today.[13]

The monk seal has probably vanished from the planet. It has been observed since antiquity on the French Mediterranean coasts. At the end of the nineteenth century it could still be seen between Nice and Banyuls, and it flourished in the Hyères Islands. The last one spotted was in Corsica in 1973.

Still found in France, the European mink is on the verge of extinction. Over the last twenty years, the Atlantic salmon population has been greatly reduced in number, victim to several problems: dams, overfishing, pollution.[14]

The coral reefs — emblematic of tropical seas, so colourful, and teeming with exotic organisms such as gorgonian coral and clown fish that can be viewed in shallow water using only a snorkel — could soon be seen by tourists only in their dreams.[15] More than a quarter have now disappeared, and the decline is continuing at an accelerated rate. Also affected are sea horses, tiny aquatic creatures of which the males transport the children.[16]

Sea tortoises are disappearing due to fishing, but also as a result of ingesting plastic bags that they mistake for jellyfish.[17]

We could go on with this sad catalogue for pages and pages.

ANIMALS, HUMANS, SAME STRUGGLE

I like animals, and wild animals in particular. In fact, one of my most recent books is called *Birds, Marvellous Birds*. I'm often on the receiving end of the classic response offered to those who speak out on behalf of animals: why work so hard for their survival when there are so many human beings experiencing great difficulty? Shouldn't we focus our energies on them?

There is no conflict between the two causes. On the contrary. We're together, in distress, on the same boat. I remember a poster in a science museum in the United States. Under the title, "Animal species that are extinct or threatened with extinction," one could see a dodo from Mauritius, a rhinoceros, a white tiger, and at the bottom ... a man, a woman, and a baby. It packed a punch.

All through our short residence on the planet, animals have been our fellow travellers. Current scientific wisdom on the workings of life underscores how interdependent we are with the living species that surround us. In fact, the entire planet is bound up in an enormous ecosystem that includes water, air, and earth, and in which each animal and plant plays a specific role.

I repeat, life is extraordinarily robust. To all appearances, it will survive, persist, and flourish beyond the current crisis. The question for us human beings is whether we will still be there, and how many species we will drag down with us when we fall. Preserving plants, animals, and humans is the same struggle, the same fight for survival.

There is another area where these same words take on a special meaning: that of individual behaviour. Compassion begins in our attitude towards animals. Implicit is our hope of seeing the warlike instincts that pervade the history of mankind reduced — instincts that gravely endanger its future now that we possess such terrifying arsenals (see Chapter 4).

I've arranged in a box a number of quotations from some of our greatest minds, from Pythagoras to Gandhi, through Leonardo da Vinci, Montaigne, and Victor Hugo. All assert that "the cruelty we show towards animals is only our apprenticeship for that we will show towards men," to quote Jacques-Henri Bernardin de Saint-Pierre.

Still, man is becoming more compassionate. The existence of a great many movements dedicated to protecting nature and animals is certainly an encouraging sign.

In past centuries, many writers and philosophers rose up against cruelty towards animals. But if I am not mistaken, organized movements[18] to defend living beings are relatively recent in the history of humanity. Their appearance is linked to our realization that human activity has done great harm to the environment, and has led to the disappearance of many species. But this demonstrates above all, the emergence of compassion for animals and a will to take concrete measures to defend them, not only from extinction, but from the cruel treatment we reserve for them.

That, it seems to me, constitutes a shift in man's sensibility that could have a very positive influence on the future history of human relations. All the more reason, I would say, to encourage and support those movements for the protection of nature.

I am myself personally involved in the defence of wild animals. A few years ago I was invited by Allain Bougrain-Dubourg to a demonstration against the illegal hunting of wood doves that fly every spring from Mauritania towards the Scandinavian countries. Like many long-distance migratory birds, they try as much as possible to fly over land rather than sea, so that they can set down if they're suffering from fatigue or hunger. This strategy leads them, as they overfly the Gironde estuary, to pass over the tip of Grave, and cross the water to Royan. There, thousands of camouflaged hunters in raised cabins lie in wait to shoot them down en masse. As a result, every year the population declines, and the Nordic countries protest vigorously.

A FEW QUOTATIONS

"As long as men massacre animals, they will kill each other. He who sows murder and pain cannot reap joy and love." — Pythagoras, 570–480 BC

"The day will come when the act of killing an animal will be condemned exactly like that of killing a human being." — Leonardo da Vinci, 1452–1519, *Prophecies*

"Those who are bloodthirsty by nature where animals are concerned have a natural inclination to cruelty." — Michel de Montaigne, 1533–1592, *Essays*

"What a pity, and how petty to claim that animals are machines deprived of knowledge and feeling." — Voltaire, 1694–1778, *Philosophical Dictionary*, "Beasts"

"Cruelty towards animals is in violation of man's duty towards himself." — Immanuel Kant, 1724–1804, *Foundations of the Metaphysics of Morals*

"Between compassion for animals and goodness of heart, there is a direct link." — Arthur Schopenhauer, 1788–1860, *On the Basis of Morality*

"You will never, under any circumstances, be wholly unhappy if you are kind to animals." — Victor Hugo, 1802–1885

"What is man without the beasts? If all the beasts were gone, men would die from a great loneliness of spirit. For whatever happens to the beasts, soon happens to man." — "Declaration to the President of the United States," attributed to the Indian Chief Seattle, 1854

"When a man wants to murder a tiger, he calls it sport; when the tiger wants to murder him, he calls it ferocity." — George Bernard Shaw, 1856–1950

"The greatness of a nation and its moral progress can be judged by the way its animals are treated." — Gandhi, 1869–1948

"A single bird in a cage, and freedom is in mourning." — Jacques Prévert, 1900–1977

"Man has little hope of ceasing to be a torturer of man as long as he continues to practise on animals his craft of executioner." — Marguerite Yourcenar, 1903–1987, August 7, 1957

Should I have accepted the invitation? I hesitated for a long time. I tend to be a bit of a coward, physically. I could just stay at home and protest in writing from my safe and comfortable office. Then, after a discussion with my wife, Camille, we decided to go together. A busload of police accompanied us. I have a horrible memory of this encounter: a few feet in front of us, dozens of hunters, some in combat gear, livid with rage, raising their fists and their guns in the air. These expressions of hatred — even if you were two steps from the bus in which you could seek refuge at any time, which is what we ended up doing — are traumatic, and have more than once jolted me awake in the middle of a nightmare.

This memory was certainly connected to my joining the ROC a few years later, an organization that defined itself as being opposed to hunting. The ROC (Rassemblement des opposants à la chasse) was founded in 1976 by Théodore Monod, a great defender of nature. On his death, I was asked to take his place. But I must say that the association's name did not please me, as I am not a dyed-in-the-wool opponent to hunting. Subsistence hunting is still a necessary occupation for some human populations, and controlled hunting can be useful when a species such as the boar multiplies to the point of causing extensive damage to a rural economy. I am against hunting for the pleasure of killing, hunting as a sport or leisure activity, because it awakens and gives expression to man's crueller instincts.

Before accepting this post, I therefore asked the ROC to change its name, and they agreed. It is now called the "League for the Preservation of Wild Animals and for the Defence of Non-Hunters." ROC has become a "logo" with no negative connotations, representing the strength of our convictions. Positive thinking, being *for* something, is more effective and constructive than a negative attitude.

The League has short- and long-term goals, and takes concrete action. It has obtained a partial modification of the Verdeille Law, which allowed hunters access to property without consent in order to stalk and shoot an animal. We also succeeded in shortening the hunting season in compliance with European directives. We obtained an interdiction against lead in hunters' gun cartridges in 2006. The increased concentration of this metal in the soil and in certain ponds is disturbing, but it's hardly a surprise when we consider that two hundred and forty million cartridges are used in France every year. Absorbed by animals, the lead moves up the food chain and causes serious lead poisoning in livestock, birds, and sometimes even humans.[19]

What is more, for electoral reasons and others, authorities tolerate illegal behaviour on the part of hunters. We make such violations known so that the laws can be enforced correctly. Hunters must also be able to recognize endangered species and should avoid hunting when there is not enough light to identify them. We therefore discourage nighttime hunting.

But hunting is not the only activity that concerns us; we also support beekeepers who defend their bees, and, more generally, we are on the side of those who protest against pesticides and other toxic substances.

Our long-term goal is more ambitious. We want hunting, which, I repeat, is a necessary activity, to separate itself from the cruel behaviour with which it has long been associated. We want to "humanize" hunting. Killing a partridge or a rabbit should no longer be regarded as a sport or a recreational pleasure.

We have reason to be optimistic on the subject. History encourages us. Two thousand years ago, under the Roman Empire, circus games were very popular. Applauded by the crowd, gladiators killed each other and lions devoured human beings. These spectacles were accepted and even highly valued. Seneca, a Roman philosopher known for his humanity, wrote humorously: "Go to the games at noon: they're bloodier. At night they're just faking!"

Today, any attempt to restore this tradition would encounter serious opposition. What happened was the gradual assimilation on a global scale of a new sensibility: we no longer kill humans for the pleasure of crowds.

Similarly, slavery was viewed as being essential to society's well-being for centuries (read Cicero). It was abolished in the name of human rights. Today's slave owners, and there are still a large number, are condemned, and often subject to legal action. The situation of women has improved in many countries, and their mistreatment is denounced internationally. These changes give us the hope and will to carry on with the humanization of being human.

Still, cruelty will always be present in the hearts of humans, and will rear its head as soon as social conditions are favourable. We have seen many instances of this, from Nazi Germany, to Rwanda, to the Balkans, and Iraq. Civilization's role is to make such cruelty socially unacceptable.

What does that have to do with hunting and hunters? Here is a telling anecdote on the subject. During the war in Serbia, television reporters interviewed a young sniper, a sensitive-looking boy who expressed himself well. He admitted to having killed, personally, from the top of a building in Sarajevo, 256 pedestrians. "And how did you develop a taste for this?" asked the reporter. "The first time," said the boy, "was when my father put a gun in my hands and took me duck hunting."

This is an extreme example of an obscure impulse present in all humans: the joy of killing. It is this impulse that civilization must learn to control. Therein resides, I repeat, the hope of one day doing away with bloody wars, massacres, and genocides.

The role of education is crucial. When a child tortures an insect or an animal, his teacher must make clear to him the barbarity of his act, and persuade him that it is wrong. Because, even if children have sadistic impulses at times, they instinctively love animals.[20] We must capitalize on this natural inclination to instill in them a respect for life, and convince them of the importance of protecting nature in all its forms. Our league has set up a network whose goal is to teach this wisdom in schools.

This "wisdom" is also that of Buddhism. Buddha preaches unconditional respect for life and an active compassion for every living thing. In our day, for example, the Dalai Lama never misses an opportunity to condemn recreational hunting. Recently, he made a public declaration denouncing trophy hunting that has been introduced into Buddhist Mongolia, under pressure from Western hunters. "It's totally contrary to the principles of Buddhism," he declared. "How can we destroy and toy with the lives of animals just for amusement, pleasure, or sport? It's unthinkable."[21]

But to return to the question of hunting in Western countries, I have the impression that the general public is coming to terms with the phenomenon, and again, I am optimistic. Many countries have taken positive action on this subject of late. Scotland, for example, has outlawed hunting, which, according to Scottish members of parliament, is "a barbaric sport that has no place in a modern and civilized Scotland."[22]

In Greenland,[23] following a dramatic drop in the populations of guillemots, eider ducks, and terns, which migrate not only to France but also Iceland and Canada, the hunting season has been significantly shortened. The Minister of the Environment added, "We would be lying to ourselves if we did not follow the advice of the scientists. We want to save these species so that future generations can profit from them." Greenland also banned the use of lead in cartridges for hunting rifles following several instances of serious poisoning of Greenlanders who had eaten birds killed with lead bullets.

Similar examples may be cited in a number of other countries, including Germany[24] and England. In France, where electoral considerations tend towards a respect for "our ancient ancestral traditions," this preoccupation is receiving very active attention.

In fact, public opinion is often in advance of public policy on this question, as a survey in Italy has recently shown.[25]

ANIMAL EXPERIMENTATION

Associations for the defence of animals have also launched campaigns against laboratory experiments that, at times, cause animals extreme suffering. These experiments often seem crucial for advancing medical knowledge, and medical experimentation aims to improve not only human health, but also that of animals. It's a complex issue that pits one way of thinking against another. The antivivisectionist faction has become increasingly radical, whereas the scientific community has evolved, and is trying to reduce the number of animals involved in experimentation and to eliminate all suffering. Too slowly, no doubt.

Experimentation must be applied only in situations where it is absolutely essential. On the one hand, it must submit to ethical rules, and researchers' training must include instruction in moral and legal obligations. On the other hand, we must hope that the development of alternative techniques will lead to its ultimate irrelevance. But it's too early to say.

Beyond issues of hunting and fishing for sport, there is, today, in

Anglo-Saxon countries, a widespread philosophical debate unfolding on the status of animals. Some affirm that we should consider animals, and even plants, as subjects with rights and not as simple objects we can buy, sell, or destroy.

Before killing a bear they had captured, the Indians of my country, Canada, excused themselves: "We have nothing to eat. It's you or us." They considered the animals as "kindred peoples" and not as "things." The whole question of animals' status must be rethought today and, along with it, humankind's place in nature.[26]

6

THE SPECTRE OF PLANETARY POVERTY

HUNGER IN THE WORLD

It would have been easy, between 1970 and 1980, to chastise environmentalists for rallying only to the cause of plants and animals and not man. But things have changed. Given the hundreds of millions of human beings living lives of extreme hardship, it has become clear that the preservation of the planet and the fight against poverty are closely linked.

Here, we are dealing with a painful subject, one we would much rather be spared. But the facts are clear. Poverty, and, above all, the gap between rich and poor, constitute, along with global warming, the gravest threat to humanity's future.

We have already seen that hunger in the world decreased during the twentieth century. All the same, every minute, somewhere on Earth, a few hours flight from our well-stocked refrigerators, fifteen people die

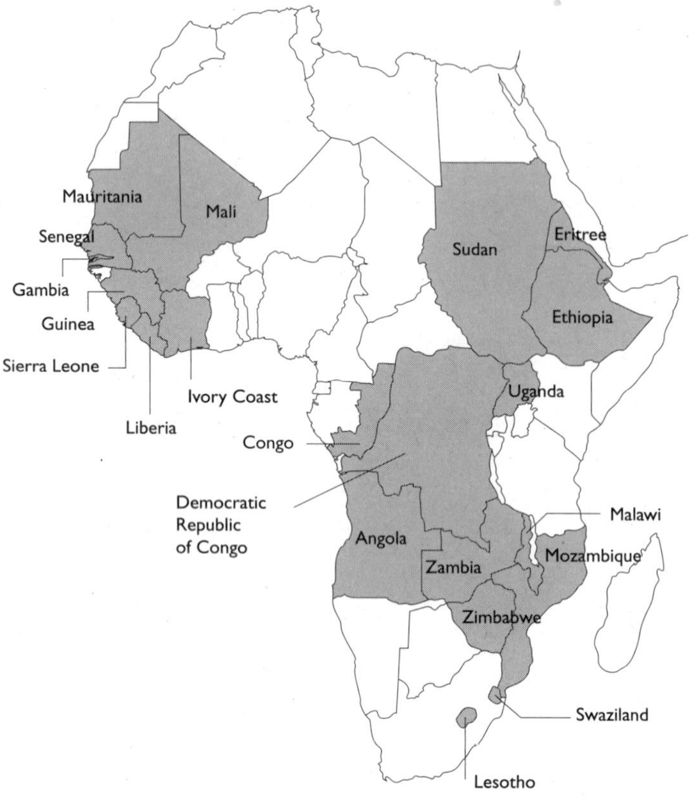

Figure 6.1. Drought and political negligence are responsible for famine in Africa. Thirty-eight million Africans are in a desperate situation. The countries in grey are the most affected.

SOURCE: *Le Monde*, 17 DECEMBER 2002.

of hunger. One human being in ten is undernourished.[1] This person has no plumbing, and must sometimes travel kilometres for water, which is often not drinkable. One human being in three lives below the poverty line, estimated at less than two dollars per day.

Africa remains the most afflicted continent, especially the sub-Saharan zone. In Somalia, 75% of the population suffers from malnutrition. In

Burundi, the Congo, Mozambique, and Angola, the rate is more than 50%. Hunger still plagues India, but also Afghanistan, Haiti, Honduras, Venezuela, and many regions in central Asia. The rural regions are the most vulnerable. There, 75% of those living in poverty are tenant farmers. It's no surprise that the statistics on health, education, and political participation are far inferior to those in urban regions (*Figure 6.1*).

POVERTY AND ENVIRONMENTAL PROBLEMS

The more people are deprived, the less able they are to contend with health problems caused by pollution or environmental disturbances. The result: they suffer disproportionately from the repercussions of environmental problems.[2]

It's impossible not to think of the eco-refugees, the millions of people forced to uproot themselves due to drought, deforestation, or flooding.

But there are distinctions to be made. Populations have always been dispersed in the wake of natural catastrophes. What is new today is that there are other contributing factors directly linked to human activity. For example: desertification due to erosion or overly intensive cultivation forces farmers to leave their lands.[3] Every year, a million Mexicans cross over to the United States for that reason. The United Nations Environment Programme (UNEP) estimates that environmental refugees number more than twenty-five million, about as many as there are political refugees. To that we must add industrial disasters (almost 400,000 people were uprooted after the Chernobyl accident), and serious climatic problems. The warming of the air, rising waters, and other calamities such as Hurricane Katrina, have caused numerous population movements.

Now, with the increase in warming, this number can only grow. The rising sea level threatens many poor and overpopulated deltas, but also tourist havens such as the Polynesian archipelago or the Falklands. A one-metre increase in the sea level would result in the exile of fifteen to twenty million people in Bangladesh, ten million in the Mekong Delta, and four million in Nigeria. Another example: the melting of Himalayan glaciers would cause a rapid rise in the water level of a dozen great lakes, which would risk flooding many Nepalese villages in the valleys.

Environmental problems therefore lead to greater poverty in the world. The poorest parts of the planet are often those most vulnerable to the impact of climatic disturbances.

On the other hand, poverty itself contributes to a deterioration of the environment. In Africa, for example, entire populations fleeing famine or massacres have found refuge in the deep forest. Species such as monkeys, big cats, and rare birds are now in great danger as a result of these massive migrations by people in distress to wild animal reserves.

In Chile, along the Pan-American Highway, I saw truckers burning old tires at night to keep warm. Huge clouds of smoke rose up, black, nauseating, and toxic.

A peasant uproots and burns trees in the Brazilian forest because he has no other way to keep warm and feed himself. The carbon dioxide generated aggravates the greenhouse effect. What is more, he is destroying the habitats of thousands of species that will disappear and never be available for medicinal purposes. It's a boomerang effect coming back to haunt us in our ivory towers, a message from the disinherited to remind us of their existence and their pain. What is certain is that all of us, rich and poor, will suffer the consequences of the greenhouse effect.

That said, it's industrialized countries that contribute the most to the production of carbon dioxide and global warming. Brazil, for example, with a population slightly less than that of the United States, produces 1.5% of the planet's emissions compared to 25% for the latter. In short, it's the richest countries that pollute the most. And it's the poorest countries that are suffering already and will suffer most dramatically in the future, especially the overpopulated countries of Southeast Asia and those of West Africa, where millions of people could be victimized by rising waters. It would seem that so long as we do not feel ourselves directly concerned, we will make no concerted effort to pollute less.

In the short term, it is certain that developing countries are much more threatened by the consequences of global warming. But in the medium and long term, as we saw at the beginning of this book, we are all implicated, and it's the whole of humanity that is in grave danger. The industrialized countries that produce most of the greenhouse gases must understand this. History shows that humans have great difficulty anticipating what is to come, and changing their way of life in the name of the precautionary principle. To return to the topic of poverty in the world, I would like once more to mention Bjørn Lomborg's book, which claims that Earth is the best of all possible worlds, that poverty has decreased more in the last fifty years than in the past five centuries, and that, as proof, life expectancy on the planet has increased from thirty to sixty-seven years during the twentieth century.[4] These statistics run counter to the alarms being raised over a growth in poverty. But let's take a closer look.

THE NORTH-SOUTH GAP

An immense gap has developed between the countries of the North and of the South, and, within these regions, between the rich and the poor. There is no famine in Europe or North America, health care has improved, and, as a result, life expectancy has increased significantly.

That is not how it is in many other countries. For lack of care and vaccinations,[5] eleven million children under the age of five die every year.

An epidemic like that of AIDS (*Figure 6.2*) provides an eloquent example.[6] While it is producing fewer and fewer deaths in the West thanks to the use of appropriate medicines, AIDS is ravaging Africa, certain Asian countries, especially China, and the former USSR. All of these are regions without access to the costly therapy that could save hundreds of millions of lives. The result: in less fortunate nations, life expectancy for humans has been going down for a decade, in particular in Africa, where it now stands at forty-five years,[7] and in the former Soviet Union.

Add to that the impact of religious authorities who continue to fight against contraception.[8] This attitude forces many women living in developing countries to give birth to unwanted children. It increases — even though it's meant to reduce them — the number of secret abor-

Year	HIV Infections in millions	Deaths in millions
1980	0.1	0.0
1981	0.3	0.0
1982	0.7	0.0
1983	1.2	0.0
1984	1.7	0.1
1985	2.4	0.2
1986	3.4	0.3
1987	4.5	0.5
1988	5.9	0.8
1989	7.8	1.2
1990	10.0	1.7
1991	12.8	2.4
1992	16.1	3.3
1993	20.1	4.7
1994	24.5	6.2
1995	29.8	8.2
1996	35.3	10.6
1997	40.9	13.2
1998	46.6	15.9
1999	52.6	18.8
2000	57.9	21.8

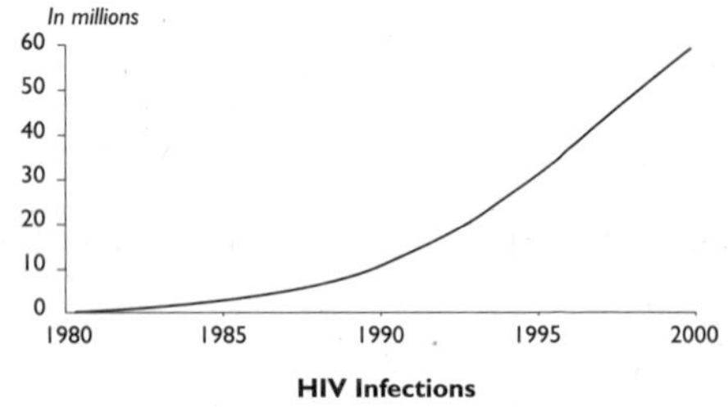

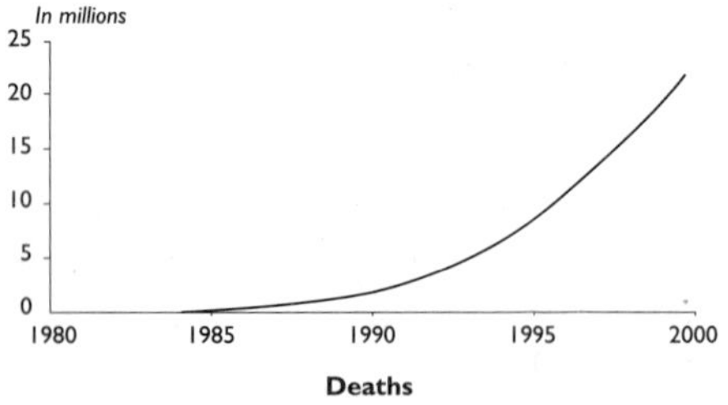

Figure 6.2. The increase of AIDS in the world since 1980. The number of HIV infections and the number of deaths.

SOURCE: *Vital Signs*, 2001, P. 79.

tions, bringing on the deaths of many mothers and increasing the mortality rate among abandoned children.

In the first decade of the twenty-first century, this gap continues to grow, and unfortunately the situation is getting worse. In 1950, the total income of the wealthiest 10% of the world's population was fifty times greater than that of the poorest 10%. In 2000, it was ninety times greater (*Figure 6.3*).

In equatorial Africa, the number of starving children has increased over the past two decades.[9] It is expected that in 2025, five out of the eight billion humans on Earth will suffer from diseases caused by water pollution (*Figure 6.4*), and that by 2050, more than 50% of the world's population will live below the poverty line. We are looking at a future where an increasingly small, increasingly wealthy population will be found behind barricades in aseptic, fortified ghettos, while a horde of the disinherited struggles to survive and ward off hunger and disease in a progressively desolate environment (*Figure 6.5*).

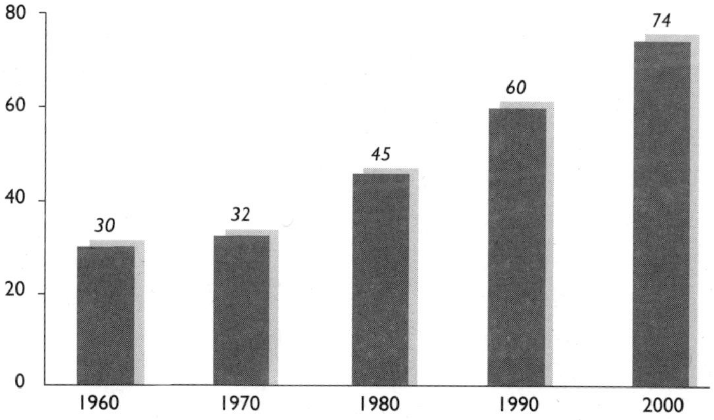

Figure 6.3. Increase in the gap in wealth since 1950. A report on the total income of the richest 10% compared to the poorest 10% of the population.

SOURCE: UNDP, *Human Development Reports*.

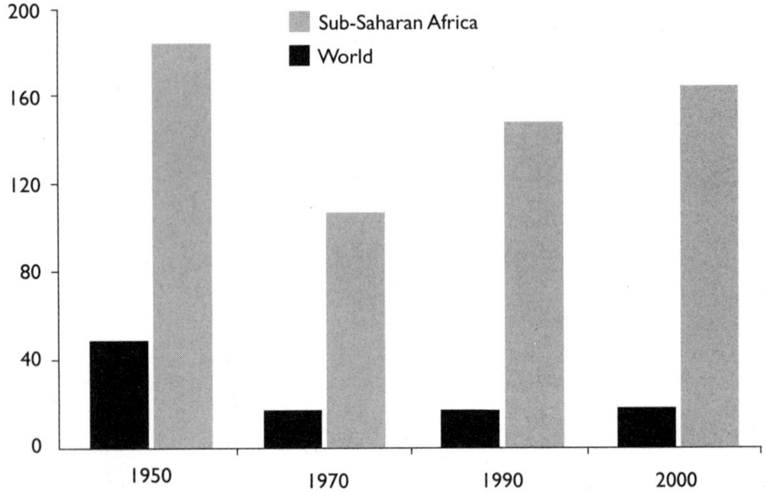

Figure 6.4. The mortality rate due to malaria per 100,000 inhabitants since 1950 in the world as a whole and in equatorial Africa in particular. After a decrease in the 1970s, the rate has been climbing steadily.

POVERTY, VIOLENCE, AND TERRORISM

This situation is inherently revolting, but it is also a source of political instability. Misery can lead to cruel dictatorships, as we saw in Germany with the rise of Nazism at the beginning of the 1930s. It is the breeding ground of violence, as we see in the suburbs of our large cities, and of terrorism in all its forms.

September 11, 2001 showed how vulnerable we are. Terrorism need not stop at bringing down skyscrapers. It could resort to measures that are even more devastating, such as nuclear, chemical, and biological weapons. By its very nature it does not consist of enemies identified with a nation, like Nazi Germany, that a global coalition could neutralize, but of a network with a thousand heads, like the Hydra, that grow back as soon as they are cut off.

No atomic arsenal, no anti-missile shield can neutralize this threat.

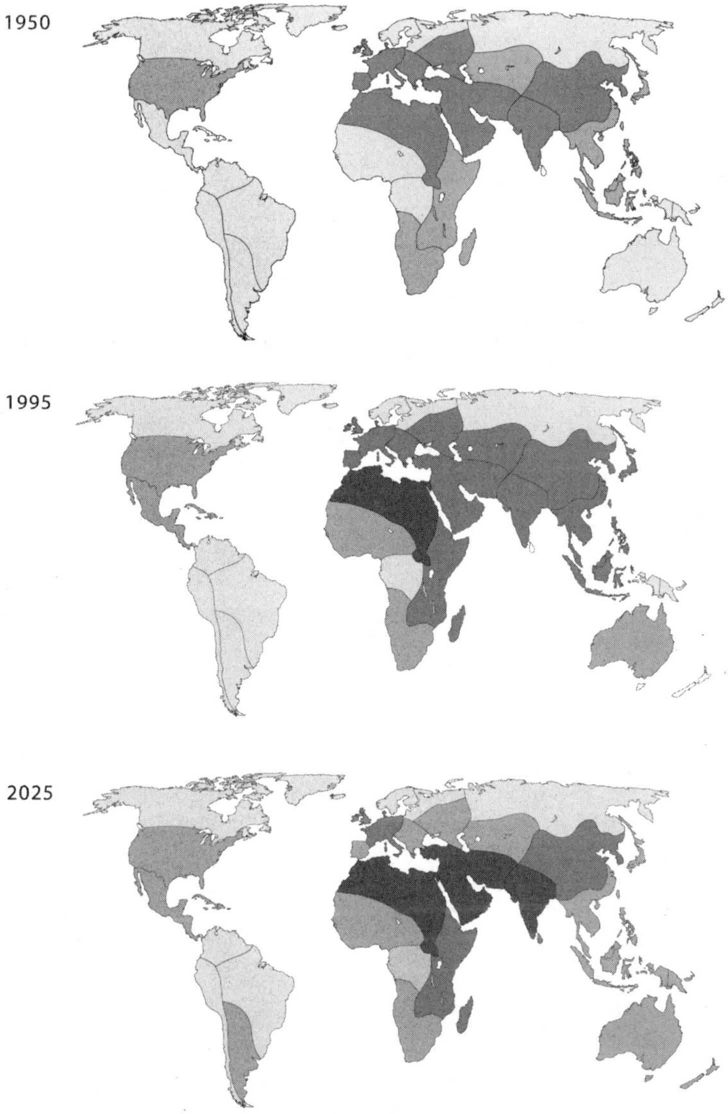

Figure 6.5. Geographical distribution of the regions where drought was the most severe in 1950 and 1995, with a projection to 2025. The darkest regions are the driest. In North Africa and the Middle East, water reserves will be eight times lower in 2025 than in 1950.
SOURCE: *Unesco Courier*, FEBRUARY 1999.

The link between poverty and terrorism is very questionable and much disputed. Those responsible for the Twin Towers attack were not poor or dispossessed. But the gulf between rich and poor countries can lay the groundwork for terrorism by inculcating a hatred of the West, and enabling terrorists to find support for their actions among destitute populations.

The poor, obviously, have neither the means nor the required organization to hijack airplanes. The most they can do, as in South Africa, is to torch and pillage shopping centres and to commit acts of vandalism. Day-to-day violence, increasingly widespread in disadvantaged suburbs around the world, reflects the resentment of those whose only future is unemployment and life in crumbling neighbourhoods. The situation is a reminder to us that poverty breeds despair, hatred, and, finally, support for terrorism. Those who have nothing, those with no future, those with only their hatred for the rich countries that exploit them, are ready-made candidates to participate in kamikaze-like attacks. And if they are not themselves poor, as was the case of the suicide bombers of bin Laden, this collective injustice feeds their mortal hatred of the West.

Radical Islamism often serves as religious and ideological sustenance for real anger and deep political and economic resentment. In any case, it is easier to blame Islamism alone for terrorism than to reflect on the underlying causes that nourish it. If we must stand firm in the face of murderous fanaticism, we must also attack the socio-economic roots of the problem and achieve a fairer division of wealth.

CHANGING OUR BEHAVIOUR

Let us first remember that about thirty developed countries represent 20% of the population, but produce and consume 85% of synthetic chemical products, 80% of non-renewable energy, 40% of fresh water, and that they emit ten times as much greenhouse gas per inhabitant than the countries of the South. All of which prompted Silvio Berlusconi to say, cynically, dismissing out of hand the effects of centuries of colonialism and neo-colonialism: "It's not the fault of the industrialized countries that they hold in their hands 80% of the world's wealth!"

Above all, profit making and the protection of our own interests must cease to be our exclusive goal if we don't want to bring ruin to entire populations at the other end of the world.

The attitude of the United States on the question of the cotton market is emblematic of what we must stop doing. World prices of cotton are falling because of the financial aid Washington provides to American cotton growers, who are producing more than ever and causing a glut on the markets. Even the *Wall Street Journal* recently denounced this behaviour: "By widening the gap between rich and poor, subsidies will create problems. Nationals from the cotton-producing countries of West Africa, where Islam is the dominant religion, are flocking massively to European cities. Those that remain are seeing more and more religious figures from Pakistan and the Middle East visiting their mosques and Koranic schools. Secular governments in Mali and neighbouring states insist that they will not allow terrorist organizations seeking to enlist the world's malcontents to transform their countries into recruitment centres, but they remind us that persistent poverty exacerbates discontent."

We can combat poverty in the world in a thousand ways. Let's begin by not creating it. That would already be something. Beyond this, there is no lack of ideas for helping poor countries resolve their problems, the first being the cancellation of their debts. The economies of poor countries are bled dry because a significant proportion of their national revenue is paid out in interest to rich countries in the name of national debt.[10]

In December 2002, the American administration refused the UN's request to send generic medicines to Africa to combat AIDS in order to protect the financial interests of its pharmaceutical industry. On the other hand, the struggle against hunger seems to have been a priority of the United Nations and many international organizations for thirty years, such as the Food and Agriculture Organization. In 1974, the FAO

Summit gave itself the goal of eradicating hunger within a decade. Twenty years later, acknowledging that the number of those starving had not gone down, this same association asked more modestly that hunger be reduced by half by 2015. In Rome, in 2002, Jacques Diouf, Director-General of the FAO, was refused by the wealthy states the 24 billion dollars he requested in order to meet that objective. The conference came to a close with no commitment from the industrialized countries. If things continue at their present pace, this reduction by half will not be achieved before 2065. At the Rio Summit, the rich countries had promised to commit 0.7% of their GNP to helping poor countries. In fact, they delivered less than 0.3%. The United States provided only 0.1%, and this figure is going down.[11]

Aid for agriculture in poor countries on the part of international authorities decreased by almost 50% between 1990 and 2000. This also directly affects advances in education, especially for women. Educated women tend to have fewer children, and are able to nourish them better. Rio called for the reduction of illiteracy by half. In fact, the number of people who neither read nor write has fallen from 25% to 21%, but the number of illiterate women has increased.

What we need is greater solidarity on the part of rich countries in relation to poor countries so that we can remedy the situation. The great challenge that faces humanity today is to put into effect lasting economic development that does not leave entire populations by the wayside, and that respects the Earth's natural balance. It's far from impossible; it simply requires concerted political will from industrialized countries.

7

TAKING ACTION

We must think globally and act locally.
René Dubos

WHAT IS TO BE DONE? That is the question we're left with after this troubling survey of the planet's condition.

Our first source of hope is people's growing concern for the planet. At one time this sentiment barely existed, but it has emerged gradually as the dangers have become clear. Thousands of years ago, no one mourned the disappearance of the Mediterranean forests, or later the extinction of the dodos in Mauritius, or of the great herds of seals and flocks of wild pigeons seen by Jacques Cartier when he arrived in Canada, around 1536.

The beginnings of environmental concern, or ecology, go back, at most, two centuries. For some decades,[1] we have been witnessing the emergence of planetary ecology, increasingly encouraged by the debates over the greenhouse effect, climatic change, and the connections between development and the environment.

On the international scale, meetings have been organized to discuss the most important problems and to seek solutions.[2]

In 1992, the Earth Summit in Rio raised a lot of hopes. Rio was at once a great disappointment[3] and an important landmark. That 107 countries decided to take the environmental problem seriously enough to gather together and seek collective solutions, was, it must be said, a signal event in the planet's history. For me, the most positive result of Rio was, thanks to television, to have introduced into the global vocabulary, at all social levels, the word "ecology." Rio made people sit up and acknowledge the real threats to our planet, and the need for planetary mobilization if we are to assure the future.

The Bali conference in 2007 and the Bonn conference in 2008 were important steps in the right direction. The important progress lies in the fact that, at Bali, decision-making people were now acknowledging the importance of global warming. At Bonn, they acknowledged the gravity of the erosion of biodiversity.

DEMOCRACIES

How can we help democracies evolve in such a way as to deal with current ecological problems in the long term? How can we make it feasible for them to undertake costly programs that stretch over decades?

"Democracy," said Churchill, "is the worst form of government, with the exception of all those others that have been tried." But where our current problems are concerned, it has the serious flaw of encouraging short-term thinking; the terms, of course, being electoral. Faced with decisions that have implications beyond their mandate — especially if the solutions require significant outlays of money that might make them unpopular — politicians have a regrettable tendency to procrastinate in order to pass the problems on to their successors. This is NIMTO once more ("not in my term of office"), a syndrome we discussed in Chapter 2.

In 2000, Al Gore, then Vice-President of the United States, and a great defender of nature, confided to President Bill Clinton, in a fateful sentence that sums up the situation in a nutshell: "The minimum [of actions, expenses, investments] that is scientifically necessary [to combat global warming] far exceeds the maximum that is politically feasible."

The president got the message, and almost nothing was done during his mandate. That didn't prevent the Democratic candidate, Al Gore, from being defeated in the 2000 elections. His successor, George W. Bush, in refusing to sign the Kyoto agreement, has been treading the same path.

Our entire political cast of mind must be changed profoundly if we want to dodge the bullet. In this connection, we must also recognize the ambivalent role of environment ministers, who, in our democracies, are too often little more than stooges for their various governments. I have had the occasion to meet several of these ministers, both in Canada and in France. Their messages are almost all the same: "If only you knew how little influence we have in the Cabinet, especially compared to Public Works and Transport."

In his masterful documentary *Forest Alert* (*L'Erreur boréale*, National Film Board of Canada), denouncing clear-cutting in the north of Quebec, the singer Richard Desjardins is told directly, by the minister himself, that his responsibilities are limited to waterways. The forest is under the complete control of the forestry companies, which are clear-cutting, unhindered, to the limits of the northern tundra.

And yet, ministers of the environment ought to be speaking out on behalf of the environmental aspirations of citizens. It is of crucial importance that their voices be heard clearly and effectively. For that, they need the support of voters as expressed through environmental protection movements. Environmentalism must provide a counterweight. In Germany, in Scandinavia, in England, citizens are involved. New hopes come from events taking place in the last few years. The film *An Inconvenient Truth* by Al Gore, the evaluation of the price of global warming (thousands of billions of dollars), and Nicolas Hulot's part in the "Grenelle de l'Environment" in France have all played an important role in pushing the protection of the environment to the front of a large number of people's minds.

NON-GOVERNMENTAL ORGANIZATIONS AND ASSOCIATIONS (NGOS)

Today, NGOs and citizens' associations are playing a crucial role in the defence of nature.

We must strongly encourage all those who are concerned with saving the planet to join them. The more powerful these associations, the more they will succeed in initiating concrete projects and influencing public policy.

Some of these groups, however, muddle the debate by exaggerating the threats, advocating unrealistic, radical solutions, or undertaking dubious actions for the benefit of the media.

We all know the saying, "The road to Hell is paved with good intentions." Radicalization and extremism are harmful to the environmental cause. But this tendency is minor compared to the wonderful work being done by associations throughout the world, and more and more today in developing countries.

SOME EXAMPLES OF CONCRETE PROGRESS

What are the most important initiatives in support of the environment that have been taken in the last decade?

I believe the most promising development for the future has been the above-mentioned realization that there is a problem and the growing interest on the part of citizens in working on behalf of the planet.

This new sensitivity to the protection of the environment is an extremely encouraging sign for the future. Yet it still has to be channelled into concrete action. Even if most of the serious problems have not been resolved, many initiatives have been taken by individuals, associations, and states.[4] We have already mentioned the banning of CFCs in order to protect the ozone layer, and the installation of catalytic converters to combat acid rain. We could also cite the progress made in cleaning up many waterways.[5]

URBAN ACTION

Many positive initiatives have already been undertaken in urban communities. One idea that is effective and aesthetically pleasing is the installation of roof gardens, as in Toronto and Chicago. This can lower the local temperature several degrees in summer, avoiding smog formation. The problems caused by automobiles have been resolved in part by cities such as Copenhagen, Denmark; Curitiba, Brazil; and Karlsruhe, Germany, by significantly improving public transport.[6] The city of Olsztyn, Poland, has set an example in energy conservation by dimming its nighttime illumination.

In another area, the coming into force of the European directives to protect wetlands has seen the British government select seventy-five wetland sites (total area: 361,000 hectares), called "Ramsar" sites,[7] and has accorded them the highest level of protection possible.

In addition, for the last fifteen years, several countries in South Asia and Oceania (China, New Zealand, the Philippines, Sri Lanka, Thailand, and Vietnam) have prohibited the exploitation of their natural forests, and are seeking the largest part of their wood supply from forestry plantations and agroforestry systems.[8]

A welcome surprise comes to us from China, whose environmental record has often left much to be desired. The construction of the Three Gorges Dam, for instance, on the Yangtze River. New Ramsar sites are being created on a regular basis. They now cover more than 24,000 square kilometres (a bit less than the area of Belgium). A centre for the protection of nature has also been opened in China to aid migratory birds suffering from pollution when they fly over urban regions.

BY THE SKIN OF THEIR TEETH

Some virtually extinct species, like the European bison or Przewalski's horse, have been saved at the last possible moment thanks to specialized centres.[9]

Many zoological parks shelter the last survivors of a number of species, and try, sometimes with success, to reintroduce them into their natural habitats. In New Zealand, one of the rarest varieties of parrot, the kakapo, was saved in the nick of time. Its population, which had been reduced to sixty-two individuals, has begun to grow rapidly. In France, the population of grouper is beginning to prosper in the protected waters of the Mediterranean.[10]

ECONOLOGY

We are also seeing the development of a green economy, or what has been called "econology." It stems from the realization that environmental measures can be profitable. The result: several industries have modified their practices with this in mind. A survey of sixty-five European businesses undertaken by a Swiss bank indicated an increase in profitability proportional to their degree of environmental commitment.[11] Far from being mutually exclusive, economic and environmental goals converge in many instances.

We have already discussed the recent development of organic agriculture, which continues to make strides. The example of the BioCoop[12] is remarkable, and shows how we can succeed in altering the rules of the economic game, and help preserve the environment and people's health.

ECOTOURISM

We can also talk about ecotourism. Nature exploration trips were very rare in the past. Only a few great explorers ventured into uncharted territory, at their own risk. One of the positive side effects of tourism is the protection host countries are prepared to offer those sites that they want to remain attractive. Many nations have discovered that catering to the camera is more profitable than making room for the gun. Elephants in Kenya may be photographed many times, but you can only shoot them once. Today, only the Japanese, the Icelanders, and the Norwegians hunt whales. The rest of the world is trying to keep them from disappearing. The fact that this species has become an object of interest for tourists is an important factor. I recently had the opportunity to visit a cross-border park, Park W, which includes parts of Niger, Benin, and Burkina Faso, in West Africa. The excursions in a dugout canoe on the Niger River, among the multicoloured birds, are enchanting. In concert with the three countries, a European commission (Ecopas), has assumed responsibility for maintaining the park. It's very much worth a visit.

Mass tourism still subjects natural environments to a great deal of stress, and contributes to the deterioration of landscapes. Wherever possible, I try to promote tourism that respects the sites visited, and their inhabitants.

I remember that when I was a student in Quebec, I went to see the whales of the Saint Lawrence River. Large herds came there to feed. They offered a magnificent spectacle, as their immense black bodies, majestic, rose from the misted water, throwing into the air their resonant spray, then vanished, barely rippling the water's surface. A few years later, visitors arriving by the hundreds on large boats began to cause the whales great distress. Strict controls were introduced, both to the number of visitors and the distance within which they could approach.

UNFORESEEN DANGERS

It's clear — and this goes beyond the issue of ecotourism — that all our actions may encounter unforeseen difficulties and worsen a situation we want to improve. The classic example is that of CFCs, those molecules destructive to the ozone layer that were initially chosen for their stability and, therefore, their non-polluting features.

Another example: in Bangladesh,[13] in an effort to irrigate the land and to provide drinkable water for the population, engineers of the British Geological Survey dug a number of wells in the Ganges delta. No one could have suspected that this operation was going to bring to the surface large quantities of arsenic contained in the sediment. Today, seventy-five million people are threatened with serious poisoning. It is always difficult to foresee the long-term consequences of an initiative or project.

Of course, tourism, even ecological tourism, can be harmful on a large scale. It must be strictly controlled. But it remains the source of a beneficial awakening. It can offer support to nature, as well as local cultures, and can play a valuable pedagogical role for all, children especially.

FOR AN ECOLOGICAL "ANTI-MANHATTAN PROJECT"

In concrete terms, what is our most urgent task?

In 1941, when we faced the threat of German and Japanese victories and the possibility of Nazi barbarism spreading around the globe, the Manhattan Project was launched with all due urgency by the United States to produce an unprecedentedly powerful weapon. An impressive number of scientific and technical experts were brought together in Los Alamos, New Mexico, and given a virtually unlimited budget. The work proceeded at a remarkable pace, and in less than four years they made scientific history. Starting from practically nothing, they produced the atomic bomb. If I draw attention to that event, it's not to discuss the relevance of the project, but to demonstrate that human beings, when faced with a serious challenge, can marshal incredible resources if the situation demands it.

The preceding chapters have outlined the serious threats weighing on our future. It is time for us to envisage projects on the scale of the Manhattan Project in the hope that investments as great and minds as powerful will be put to work as rapidly as possible. If not ...

ENERGY

We urgently need to develop all forms of renewable energy so that they can meet our end-of-century deadline. At the same time, we must considerably reduce our energy consumption by expanding our rail networks and putting in place transport systems that require less energy and cause fewer accidents. Three-quarters of the carbon dioxide responsible for global warming is produced by cars and trucks.

We must halt unreasonable deforestation, and replant trees to stop the expansion of desert and sterile zones.[14] We must revive wetlands to absorb rainfall and combat flooding.

After establishing in the last decade the right to international intervention on humanitarian grounds, we must now introduce, as Jean-Marie Pelt has suggested, a right to ecological intervention in the case of a major catastrophe.[15]

To combat hunger, agriculture must be radically transformed. We must provide security of nourishment for the hungry billions around the world. We must use incentives to develop an organic agriculture that does not use chemical products. We must put an end to monocultures. We must favour a return to agricultural products native to each region. We must revive ancestral techniques for nurturing soil and bodies of water. We must buy organic and encourage equitable trade:[16] each purchase is a vote for or against multinational control of world trade.

But it is clear that all the measures envisaged for putting the brakes on the deterioration of the planet will be futile unless we eradicate poverty and famine. Rather than preparing for the notorious and extremely costly "Star Wars," we must initiate a true campaign against poverty with increased, authentic international aid, demonstrating a real concern for all human beings.[17]

INDIVIDUAL ACTIONS

Individually, we can each undertake a number of concrete measures.[18] We are responsible for our immediate environment, a fact we must pass on to our children.

On the social level, we can join forces with movements committed to protecting the natural world.[19]

In short, it is urgent that we develop an "ecological globalization" that can effectively combat the wrongdoing and the pollution resulting from the new globalization of the economy.

8

HOW THINGS HAVE EVOLVED, 2003–2005

THE FIRST EDITION OF *Mal de Terre* appeared in April 2003. How has the situation evolved since then? This afterword constitutes a first assess-ment. A survey of the last eighteen months shows that things are changing much faster than we could have foreseen, in ways that are both negative and positive.

In humanity's distant past, nothing happened quickly. The time scale was millenial. At the end of the Middle Ages, an acceleration began to make itself felt, first on the scale of centuries and then, after the Second World War, on a scale of decades. Now the phenomenon is being felt from one year to the next. We are in a critical period, and we do not know what will prevail, the positive or the negative. It is impossible to predict the state of the planet in fifty years, or even less.

Some warning signals are changing from red to bright red, including those concerning temperature, emissions of carbon dioxide, pollution, the exhaustion of natural resources, and the erosion of biodiversity. At the same time, the Earth's population is starting to react. Thirty years ago, such widespread awareness of the gravity of our situation would have been unthinkable. International conferences are taking place, protests are being made, and, even more constructive, a will to protect the planet is galvanizing citizens' associations and is having an impact on the political world. New legislation is being passed. There is a proliferation of initiatives in the area, for example, of recycling. If those plundering the planet are making gains, so are its defenders.

The fundamental question remains: will our present planetary crisis, widely referred to as the "sixth extinction," be brought to an end thanks to determined action on the part of Earth-dwellers, or will it culminate in our extinction? The ball is still in our court. But for how long?

To keep our spirits up, let us first deliver some good news. It applies to France, but could, in the future, involve other countries. It concerns the spring 2004 adoption of the Environmental Charter; soon, it is hoped, to be accorded constitutional status. This charter incorporates the precautionary principle, and should ensure that certain disasters, such as those caused in the past by asbestos, will never recur. In fact, the precautionary principle has become indispensable, which means there will be more research undertaken to discover and refine innovations respectful of nature and our environment.

Let us pass in review, one by one, the principal problems, and assess the current situation in each case. It will be more a matter of snapshots than a comprehensive appraisal.

A) THE PLANET'S TEMPERATURE

The increase in annual average temperature has risen from 0.6 to 0.8°C since the beginning of the industrial era. 2003 was the hottest year since the climate was first studied. The effects of warming have been felt around the globe.

The polar regions have been particularly affected. Open water has supplanted ice. The melting of glaciers accelerates year after year.

Computer modelling has enabled us to anticipate climate destabilization. Extreme examples are increasingly frequent, as the last two years demonstrate. In western Europe, the 2003 heat wave caused the death of about 15,000 people, refuting those who, like Bjørn Lomborg, assert that "heat has never killed anyone."

Still in 2003, the heat triggered a boom in air conditioner sales. The laws of thermodynamics dictate that these devices throw off many more calories than they extract from the spaces they cool (cars or homes), thus contributing to the warming of the atmosphere.

Other consequences of the heat wave: ozone pollution broke all records since measurements began. In 2004, the hurricanes that came in waves were among the most damaging ever experienced. The rise in temperature triggered intense rains. Torrential rains caused massive flooding in China, America, and even France, while in Australia drought spread.

To sum up: the list of major climatic disturbances that we can, with great justification (but with no absolute certainty), attribute to global warming continues to grow. The most trustworthy computer models foresee a warming of about three degrees, perhaps more, in Europe.

B) CARBON DIOXIDE

We now know that carbon dioxide is the principal cause for the greenhouse effect, and yet the quantity of CO_2 emissions continues to increase, with the years 2002 and 2003 breaking all records. By February 2005, the Kyoto Accord had been ratified. But it only aims to reduce emissions by 6% by 2012, far from the 60% required for climate stabilization. The average consumption of motorized vehicles has risen from 10 litres per hundred kilometres to 11. This is the opposite of what should be happening. Truck transport is still being given priority, even though rail transport would be preferable. Air tickets are often cheaper than train fares, despite the fact that planes produce much more CO_2.

Thanks to governmental action, drivers have reduced their speed, a development that is saving human lives. Analogous measures must be taken that will persuade drivers to choose more energy-efficient vehicles, thereby sparing future generations enormous problems.

C) THE EXHAUSTION OF OIL

Since 2002, oil companies have begun to face the facts concerning our reserves of fossil fuel. One acknowledges that the rate at which we have discovered new sources has been diminishing for several decades. Another reduces its estimates of existing reserves. And it is expected that between 2010 and 2020 the demand will exceed the supply and the price of oil will rise inexorably. Serious economic upheavals will follow for all countries, especially those with no alternatives in place. The price increase in 2004 due to an unfavourable geopolitical situation was both bad and good news. It was bad news for those making their living driving taxis and transport vehicles, especially in poor countries, but it was good news because other energy sources, the costs of which seem too high compared to oil, will lose this handicap. Biofuels will come into their own in the world of agriculture. Their cultivation should be pesticide free in order to give them a perfectly clean slate. It should not be forgotten as well that hydrogen may become a fuel for the future.

D) SOLAR ENERGY

Here, at least, is an area where the news is good. Windmills are proliferating. On a global scale, they are providing energy equivalent to that of forty nuclear reactors (40 gigawatts), eight times more than in

1995. The widespread view that renewable energy can only play a supporting role is becoming increasingly untenable. Germany, for instance, is already supplying 10% of its electrical needs thanks to alternative technologies, and Navarre, 35%. One study indicates that offshore windmills could satisfy Europe's residential electrical needs by 2020. Local difficulties, such as the NIMBY factor and administrative complications, have delayed installation in France. But attitudes are changing, and we can be optimistic. The drawbacks of these installations are much less serious than those of oil derivatives or nuclear energy.

E) POLLUTION

The situation is deteriorating. According to a 2003 UNICEF report, more than 1.6 million children die each year from infections related to polluted water, the only water available to them. In a number of regions in France, tap water can no longer be regarded as drinking water, as it is not recommended for pregnant women or infants.
But some intelligent initiatives have been taken.

- The proportion of lead in the air has been reduced by two-thirds since the introduction of non-leaded fuel for automobiles.
- In the Japanese city of Fukuoka, all new buildings must include a system of non-drinking water so that rain water and recycled water may be used.
- Ireland has reduced its usage of single-use plastic bags by 90%. Other islands have done away with them altogether.
- Residents of Massachusetts have reduced the amount of waste released into the environment by 90%.
- The Stockholm Accord, which bans a number of chemical products, including certain pesticides, came into effect in 2004.

F) THE EROSION OF BIODIVERSITY

This is a dark area. The Seventh Conference of the Parties to the Convention on Biological Diversity (COP-7) in Kuala Lumpur, Malaysia, took place in February 2004. It brought together the representatives of the 188 parties to the United Nations Framework Convention on Biological Biodiversity, signed in Rio in 1992 at the Planet Earth summit. The goal was to adopt measures that would significantly reduce the rate of decline in biodiversity by 2010. According to the European Union, the application of the United Nations International Convention on Biodiversity is encountering serious difficulties. The destruction of species is continuing. According to the *Comité français de l'Union Mondiale pour la Nature*, France ranks fifth in the world for the number of species threatened. It bears great responsibility, especially in Guyana, New Caledonia, and Réunion.

More encouraging news:

- China wants to establish a network of nature reserves.
- Iceland seems willing to abandon the whale hunt.
- The wolf, which has been reintroduced into Yellowstone Park in the United States, is playing a major role in enriching biodiversity.
- In the United States, salt marshes on the Atlantic Coast are being restored.
- In Africa, Rwanda is taking concrete steps to preserve its flora and fauna.
- In France, residents of the Pyrenees are celebrating the bear, which they do not want to see disappear, and an increasing number of communes are taking action to protect the wilderness.
- Paris has adopted a charter of biodiversity.
- Associations for the defence of nature and the environment are multiplying, and becoming more and more effective.

G) POVERTY IN THE WORLD

The efforts on the part of poor countries to sell their products on the international market have come up against a serious obstacle: the subsidies paid by rich countries, Europe and the USA, to their farmers. In 2003, a World Trade Organization conference tried to resolve this problem. It was a failure. However, no one can ignore the fact that to maintain people in a state of desperate poverty is to provide fertile territory for terrorist leaders seeking to recruit suicide bombers.

H) WORLD POPULATION

The birth rate continues to decline across the world, including in the poorest countries. Estimates are for a ceiling no greater than nine billion for mid-century, followed by a decline.

Reasons to hope and reasons to despair. We must act in such a way that the former increase and the latter decrease. Then, hope will prevail with no constraints.

EPILOGUE

IN THE TWENTIETH CENTURY, THE Existentialists put forward the idea that man was a stranger in the universe. That he was superfluous. A kind of blight. Since that time, new scientific knowledge, the discovery of the big bang, the decoding of the universe's history from the initial chaos until the appearance of life on Earth, have refuted this view of the world. We now know that we are part of a history that spans fifteen billion years, that our presence implies the prior existence of numberless stars made up of atoms, and galaxies made up of stars.

This sense of belonging gives an extra dimension to human existence. It no longer represents a simple and fleeting episode, but a chapter in this glorious history. It imposes upon us a great responsibility: that of ensuring the survival of consciousness and intelligence on Earth.

This book, along with many others, poses a crucial question: is this increasing complexity, which we can trace all through the history of the universe, viable? Fifteen billion years of evolution have produced a being able to unearth the origins of the universe that gave it life, able to decode the behaviour of atoms and galaxies, to explore the solar system, to master the forces of nature, but unable to marshal its resources in such a way as to avert its own elimination. That, in brief, is our drama today.

It is likely that biospheres such as ours exist in great numbers across the universe. The hypothesis of the appearance of life on other planets, its evolution towards increasingly complex organisms, culminating in the appearance of intelligence in one form or another, is, of course, a matter for speculation, but is in no way implausible.

Imagine for a moment that what happened on Earth has occurred in thousands, millions, even billions of places. Extraterrestrials develop ways of living, warm themselves, emit carbon dioxide (the laws of physics, we know, are the same everywhere in the universe), discover nuclear energy, etc. Eventually, when their natural resources are exhausted, they face a crisis similar to that confronting us today.

Imagine, then, that a squad of interplanetary spacecraft undertakes a survey of planets orbiting around stars. What would they find? There, where local intelligence has succeeded in putting right earlier instabilities, they would land on a green planet and would discover marvels of creativity that nature still has in store. (The creations of Bach and van Gogh did not exist on our planet four centuries ago.)

On other planets, however, they would discover polluted soil and chemical and radioactive waste attesting to the failure of these populations.

I have chosen this image to underline the cosmic dimensions of the crisis we are undergoing. It is complexity's future on its highest plane: intelligence, consciousness, and artistic creativity that are at stake on our planet today.

A POSITIVE ASPECT OF THE CURRENT CRISIS

In a storm, when the ship is threatening to sink, the sailors, forgetful of their conflicts and quarrels, work together to try to save the vessel. The human mobilization that is coming to the fore today on a global scale is already a positive sign for the current crisis.

To become aware of the human role in this cosmic odyssey is to lend meaning to life. Following the disappearance of our twentieth-century social ideologies, this new cause could generate new enthusiasm, especially among the young. Let us hope that it will give rise to a new sense of our identity as Earth-dwellers, beyond nationalism, racism, and sexism.

Complexity and intelligence can be viable. It depends on us. That is a vital message for the generations to come.

ACKNOWLEDGEMENTS

I WOULD LIKE TO OFFER MY warmest thanks to Iolande Cadrin-Rossignol, Yves David, Nelly Boutinot, Priscilla Telmon, Robert Klapish, Yves Lancelot, Benoit Reeves, Yves Nifaker, Christophe Aubel, Martin Aubel, Claude Buret, and Roland Deleplace for their help.

H.R.

NOTES

General Bibliography

S. T. Pimm, *The World According to Pimm*, New York, McGraw Hill, 2001.

P. H. Raven, L. R. Berg and G. B. Johnson, *Environment*, Philadelphia, Saunders College Publishing, 1995.

V. Smil, *Biology on the Global Scale. The Earth's Biosphere: Evolution, Dynamics and Change*, Cambridge, MIT Press, 2002.

E. O. Wilson, *The Future of Life*, New York, Knopf, 2002.

For the most recent figures, see the annual publications of the World Watch Institute (*Vital Signs* and *The State of the Planet*) and the site http://www.worldwatch.org.

Prologue: The Future of Life on Earth

1 The "precautionary principle" as defined by the United Nations in 1994, reads as follows: "When an activity raises threats of harm to human health

or the environment, precautionary measures should be taken even if some cause and effect relationships are not fully established scientifically."

2 Let us take for example the warnings concerning the future of the biosphere. Our awareness of this problem goes back to the 1960s. In her famous book, *Silent Spring*, Rachel Carson voiced great concern at the widespread use of a new pesticide, DDT, which in her mind was going to exterminate birds and poison millions of people.

In 1968, according to Lamont Cole, an ecologist at Cornell University, the combustion of fossil fuels was going to deplete atmospheric oxygen to the point of rendering the air unbreathable.

In his book *The Population Bomb*, published in 1968, Paul Ehrlich predicted that smog (atmospheric pollution created by burning coal) was going to kill tens of thousands of people, that India would suffer from massive famines, and that before the year 2000 the ocean waters would be toxic and empty of fish.

These catastrophes, fortunately, did not occur as predicted. But the declarations played an important role in what ensued. Thanks in part to Carson's book, the use of DDT has been largely prohibited, even if its effects are still in evidence (see Chapter 3). Cole was wrong: burning fuel does not reduce the oxygen in the air, but produces the greenhouse effect and heats up the planet. His warning had the happy consequence of exposing this other problem, one of great seriousness. The Indian famines predicted by Ehrlich were avoided thanks to the green revolution, but India, having doubled its population, faces the future with much less forest and arable land. The oceans have not been emptied of fish to the extent described by Ehrlich, but many species (see Chapter 3) have been depleted to the point where their fishing has been prohibited.

The "alarmists" have sometimes been wrong or have exaggerated the problems, but they have played an important role in sounding alarms that needed to be sounded.

3 Studies of corresponding geological strata have revealed particles of soot, which suggests that forest fires ensued on a planetary scale, destroying many vegetable species. These were succeeded by opaque clouds of soot. The ozone layer may very well have been eliminated.

4 Today, we suspect more ancient meteorites of having caused the earlier great extinctions. See Luann Becker, "Repeated blows (Did extraterrestrial collisions capable of causing widespread extinctions pound the earth not

once, but twice — or even several times?)," *Scientific American*, March 2002, p. 25.

5 "The average global sea level rose 10 to 25 centimetres during the twentieth century." (Source: *Science*, 26 October 2001, p. 840.)

Cécile Cabanes, Amy Cazenave, and Christian Le Provost, "Sea level rise during past 40 years determined from satellite and in situ observations," *Science*, vol. 294, 26 October 2001, p. 840.

We have observed an average rise of 3.2 millimetres per year between 1993 and 1998 (caused primarily by the thermic expansion of water, but also by the melting of polar ice). B. C. Douglas and W. R. Peltier, "The puzzle of global sea-level rise," *Physics Today*, March 2002, p. 35.

Anthony A. Arendt, Keith A. Echelmeyer, William D. Harrison, et al., "Rapid wastage of Alaska glaciers and their contribution to rising sea level." (They [Alaska glaciers] form the largest glaciological contribution to rising sea level yet measured), *Science*, vol. 297, 19 July 2002, p. 382–385.

6 Gian-Reto-Walther, Eric Post, Peter Convey, et al., "Ecological responses to recent climate change," *Nature*, vol. 416, 28 March 2002, p. 389–395.

Jospeh Peñuelas and Iolanda Filella, "Responses to a warming world," *Science*, vol. 294, 26 October 2001, p. 793–795.

C. D. Harwell, et al., "Climate warming and disease disks for terrestrial and marine biotas," *Science*, vol. 296, 21 June 2002, p. 2158.

7 J. T. Houghton, et al. (under the direction of), *The Scientific Bases*, Cambridge, Cambridge University Press, 2001. See the chapter "Climate Change 2001."

The American government has subsequently asked its Academy of Sciences to produce an evaluative report on climate change and, more specifically, on the reliability of the IPCC report. The scientific committee of the Academy of Sciences, made up of a dozen eminent meteorologists and climatologists, confirmed the reliability of the IPCC in a report published at the end of 2001.

8 A report by the United Nations Environment Program, "Global Environmental Outlook-3 (GEO-3)." (Source: Virginia Gewin, "U.N. predicts long wait to repair environment," *Nature*, vol. 417, 30 May 2002, p. 475.)

9 "The planet is heating up at an accelerated pace: its average temperature has climbed since 1976 at a rhythm three times as rapid as that which prevailed during the previous century. The nine hottest years have been recorded since 1990."

10 John Reilly, Peter H. Stone, Chris E. Forest, et al., "Uncertainty and climate change assessments," *Science*, vol. 293, 20 July 2001, p. 430–433.

11 Are we heading towards a new ice age? See Richard B. Alley, *The Two Mile Time Machine: Ice Cores, Abrupt Climate Change, and our Future*, Princeton University Press, 2000. Richard B. Alley, "On thickening ice?" *Science*, vol. 295, 18 January 2002, p. 451–452.

12 Extremophiles include photosynthetic bacteria, microscopic invertebrates, mushrooms, and moss that are found in cold and dry Antarctic environments. There are also the specialized microbes that live in the ocean's volcanic chimneys at temperatures close to the boiling point of water, and marine organisms that survive pressures a thousand times greater than atmospheric pressure. Other organisms thrive at altitudes much higher than that of Mount Everest.

13 The Earth and Venus contain about the same amount of carbon in their surface layers. On our planet, almost all carbon atoms are trapped at the bottom of oceans, incorporated into sedimentary stones (carbonates), while the atmosphere contains a tiny fraction (a few millionths) in the form of carbon dioxide.

Why this difference? Because of the presence of liquid water on the Earth's surface. The plankton of the ocean layers transforms the CO_2 into marine sediments. Due to its elevated surface temperature (460°C), Venus has no liquid water, and the carbon stays in the atmosphere. One last question presents itself: is it a fact that on Venus, closer to the sun than the Earth, solar heat has prevented the appearance of a layer of water? The question remains controversial.

14 A study published in 1992 shows that the average number of spermatozoa in human sperm decreased by 45% between 1940 and 1990. (Source: R. Sharye and N. Shakkebaeck, *Lancet*, no. 341.) "Sperm counts dropping," *Vital Signs*, 1999, p.148. T. Colborn, D. Dumanoski, and J.P. Meyers (under the direction of), *L'homme en voie de disparition?* Paris, Terre vivante, 1998.

Among the impossible to predict factors that could accelerate the deterioration of the biosphere, there is the possibility of new wars. The development of technologies will provide them greater destructive power than in the past. Imagine what the twentieth century's world wars would have left behind if atomic, chemical, and bacteriological weapons had been more widely used.

15 Crispin Tickell, "Communicating climate change (requires leadership,

agitation, and a catastrophe or two)," *Science*, vol. 297, 2 August 2002, p. 737.

Bibliography

B. Lomborg, *The Skeptical Environmentalist. Measuring the Real State of the World*, Cambridge, Cambridge University Press, 2001.

P. H. Raven, "Science, sustainability and the human prospect," *Science*, 9 August 2002, p. 954.

V. Smil, *Biology on the Global Scale. The Earth's Biosphere: Evolution, Dynamics and Change*, Cambridge, MIT Press, 2002.

E. O. Wilson, *The Future of Life*, New York, Knopf, 2002.

E. O. Wilson, *Scientific American*, January 2002.

Internet Site

Fondation Nicolas Hulot: http://www.fnh.org

1 Change of Air, Change of Era.

1 It was Jean Baptiste Joseph Fourier who, in 1824, realized the importance of the natural greenhouse effect to the warming of our atmosphere. A little later, fearing the return of an ice age, the Swiss chemist Nicolas-Théodore de Saussure imagined that the emission of CO_2 from huge fires might delay such a catastrophe.

Towards the end of the nineteenth century, John Tyndall and Olaf Arrhenius discovered the role carbon dioxide and water vapour played in this phenomenon. Since then, we have learned about other greenhouse gases, such as methane (CH_4), nitrogen dioxide (NO_2), and different varieties of chlorofluorocarbons (CFCs) produced by human industry (CCl_3F, called CFC-11, and CCl_2F_2, called CFC-12).

Compared to CO_2, the capacity to absorb heat, in terms of mass, is as follows: CO_2 = 1; CH_4 = 70; NO_2 = 200; low-altitude ozone = 1,800; CFC-11 = 4,000; CFC-12 = 6,000.

Today, the atmosphere contains about 800 billion tonnes of CO_2, 3.4 of methane, and 0.6 of NO2. The average times these gases remain in the atmosphere before disappearing are: CO_2 = 120 yrs; CH_4 = 10 yrs; NO_2 = 150 yrs. Since 1900, the concentration of greenhouse gases in the atmosphere has increased: CO_2 has risen from 280 to 385 (in 2008) parts per million — ppm — (in fractions of mass), CH_4 from 0.8 to 1.72 ppm, NO_2 from 0.29 to 0.31 ppm. (Source: "Carbon Emissions reaches new high," *Vital Signs*, 2001, p. 52.) According to "Certainly warmer," *Journal of Climatology*, (vol. 15, 2002, p. 3117, and *Science*, 18 October 2002, p. 497), to double the quantity of CO_2 beyond the preindustrial level (280 ppm) would lead, with a probability of 95%, to an increase of at least 1.6°C.

2 Studies on the isotopic abundance of water in zircon crystals show that water began to condense during the first millions of years of the Earth's existence. See *Geology*, No. 30, 2002, p. 351.

3 These dates have been contested. C. Fedo and M. Whitehouse, "Metasomatic Origin of Quartz-Pyroxene Rock, Akilia, Greenland, and Implications for Earth's Earliest Life," *Science*, vol. 296, 2002, p. 1448.

4 James F. Kasting, "The rise of atmospheric oxygen," *Science*, vol. 293, 3 August 2001, p. 819. U. H. Wiechert, "Earth's Early Atmosphere," *Nature*, 20 December 2002, p. 2341.

Methane would have played an important role as a greenhouse gas in the atmosphere's infancy. Methanogenic bacteria would have sequestered carbon by mineralizing it (mineralization of organic matter during the Archaean Era, 3800–2500 Ma). The atmosphere of Titan, a satellite of Saturn, could be considered a prototype for the Earth's atmosphere.

5 The fluctuations in sunlight due to variations in the Earth's orbit are too weak to explain on their own discrepancies of more than 5°C between the warm and the glacial periods. They trigger the cycle, and its effect is amplified by the behaviour of both water and carbon dioxide. The main point is the following: cold water can dissolve more carbon dioxide than warm water. Therefore, when the Earth's surface becomes warmer, the ocean depths become less efficient and the balance in temperature between the source of CO_2 (volcanoes) and the depths (the ocean) steadily grows, increasing, in turn, the quantity of carbon dioxide. Note that this balance between temperature, carbon dioxide, and methane is very slow to establish itself. This slowness is at the root of our current troubles.

6 A. Berger and M. F. Loutre, "An exceptionally long interglacial ahead?" *Science*, vol. 297, 23 August 2002.

7 In depth, temperature soundings confirm a warming trend over the last fifty years; see Hugo Beltrami et al., *Geophysical Res. Lett.*, 29, 8-1, 2002. S. T. Giles, "Warming of the Southern Ocean since the 1950s," *Science*, 15 February 2002, p. 1275. *Vital Signs*, 2001, p. 51.

8 Rasmus Benestad, "Don't blame it on the sunshine," *Physics World*, July 2001, p. 19.

9 The annual quantity of carbon emitted by fossil fuels has grown from 2 GtC (billions of tonnes of carbon) in 1955, to 6.5 GtC in 2001. Add to that the emissions caused by deforestation and agriculture, and we arrive at a total of 9 GtC. Today, the oceans and vegetation absorb only half of these emissions. The rest accumulates in the atmosphere and adds to the greenhouse effect. At this rate, by 2100, atmospheric CO_2 will double, compared to its cumulative preindustrial level (620 Gt).

The carbon dioxide in our atmosphere ultimately derives from the erosion of limestone and volcanic emissions. Absorbed by sea water, it is then incorporated into carbonates that settle on the ocean floor. (The molecules of CO_2 dissolve in water and serve as food for planktonic organisms. A small fraction of the carbonated bodies sink down to become limestone.) In this way, carbon atoms participate in the movements of the Earth's crust, and are again emitted into the atmosphere through erosive and volcanic activity.

In the past, concentrations that remained in the atmosphere altered slowly over time. Vegetation on land and in the sea absorbed and gave off CO_2 (the growth of plants and the decomposition of dead plant life). There was a constant exchange between the CO_2 absorbed and given off by living things. A balance was achieved that was a function of the ambient temperature: warm water absorbs less carbon dioxide than cold water. We see once more how temperature variations are related to variations in the concentration of carbon dioxide. (Source: "Soot takes Center Stage," *Science*, 27 September 2002, p. 2214.)

10 "Carbon sequestration by land plants cannot be relied on as a substitute for emissions reductions," *Geophysical Research Letters*, No. 29, 2001, p. 10. See also: "Carbon sinks," *Science*, 19 April 2002; Dan Ferber, "Superweeds, and a sinking on carbon sinks," *Science*, vol. 293, 24 August 2001, p. 1425; Eric A. Davidson and Adam I. Hirsch, "Fertile forest experiments," *Nature*, vol. 411, 24 May 2001, p. 431.

Jorge L. Sarminento and Nicolas Gruber, "Sinks for anthropogenic carbon," *Physics Today*, August 2002, p. 30–36.

11 Sallie W. Chisholm, Paul G. Falkowski, and John J. Cullen, "Discrediting ocean fertilization," *Science*, vol. 294, 12 October 2001, p. 309.

"Norway sinks ocean carbon study," *Nature*, September 2002, p. 6.

"The Oresmen: on fertilising the ocean," *Nature*, 9 January 2003, p. 109.

Virginia Gewin, "Ocean carbon study to quit Hawaii," *Nature*, vol. 417, 27 June 2002, p. 888.

12 Thomas M. Smith, Thomas R. Karl, and Richard W. Reynolds, "How accurate are climate simulations," *Science*, vol. 296, 19 April 2002, p. 483–484.

T. M. L. Wigley and S. C. B. Raper, "Interpretation of high projections for global-mean swarming," *Science*, vol. 293, 20 July 2001, p. 451–454.

13 El Niño, also known as "Austral oscillation," is a climatic event that occurs about every five years in the South Pacific Ocean. Due to a complex meteorological phenomenon, a warm current crosses the Pacific from west to east, and at the end of the year (Christmas) reaches the South American coast, where it was named "the little child" by Peruvian fishermen. In 1997, El Niño took on unusual proportions; it generated torrential rains in South America and a massive drought in Indonesia, which caused huge fires. There was much thought given to the link between the increased warming of the ocean current and the warming of the air. It's still too soon to give a definitive answer, but the connection cannot be ruled out. In 1997, El Niño was responsible for the record sum of 32 billion dollars in damage. Since then, insurers have become the most enthusiastic supporters of ecological action.

14 C. Drew Harvell, Charles E. Mitchell, R. Jessica Word, et al., "Climate warming and disease risks for terrestrial and marine biota," *Science*, vol. 296, 21 June 2002, p. 2158–2162.

Jonathan A. Patz, et al., "Regional warming and malaria resurgence," *Nature*, vol. 420, 12 December 2002, p. 627–628.

A study by the National Center for Ecological Analysis and Synthesis in Santa Barbara: "A warmer world but also a sicker one."

More than a million deaths per year are caused by malaria. Half a billion people catch it each year. (Source: "Malaria's lethal grip tightens," *Vital Signs*, 2001, p. 134.)

Climatic change has enabled mosquitoes in Africa to occupy new ecological niches, in particular at higher altitudes. We find mosquitoes at an altitude of over 2,500 metres in regions where that had never before occurred. (Source: Yves Lancelot, personal communication.)

15 The disappearance of the polar regions could slow the circulation of ocean currents and alter, in particular, the flow of the Gulf Stream, which tempers the European climate. The increase in rainfall at higher latitudes

reduces the salinity of sea water. That, added to warming, reduces the density of polar water and slows its sinking to the bottom of the polar sea, a phenomenon that drives the conveyor belt that redistributes solar heat. Bob Dickson, Igor Yashayaev, Jens Meinke, et al., "Rapid freshening of the deep North Atlantic Ocean over the past four decades," *Nature*, vol. 416, 25 April 2002, p. 832–836.
Clark P. U., et al., "The role of thermohaline circulation in abrupt climate change," *Nature*, 21 February 2002, p. 863.

16 The regions of permafrost in the Northern Hemisphere contain 390 Gt of methane sequestered in the ice. The freeing of a small fraction of this gas could have a disastrous impact on global warming. It must be remembered that, for an equal concentration, methane contributes about seventy times more to global warming than CO_2.

Indigo A. Pecher, "Gas hydrates on the brink," *Nature*, vol. 420, 12 December 2002, p. 622–623.

Peter Clift and Karen Bice, "Baked Alaska — the heating of sediment in the Gulf of Alaska as an important source of the greenhouse gas methane," *Nature*, vol. 419, 12 September 2002, p. 129–130.

http://www.bghrc.com/CentreNews/Newsletters/Alert6_Summer2002 web.pdf

17 James F. Kasting and Janet L. Siefert, "Life and the evolution of Earth's atmosphere," *Science*, vol. 296, 10 May 2002, p. 1066–1067.

18 Observations in Canada have shown that the thickness of the ozone layer greatly decreased over the Arctic towards the end of the 1990s, especially in early spring of 1997.

19 CFCs are chlorofluorocarbons. It is a particularly stable molecule because it contains two atoms that tend to create powerful bonds: chlorine and fluorine. Its stability enables it to react very weakly with other atoms. That is its strength and its weakness. The molecules accumulate in the air and reach the high atmosphere. There, they are broken down by the sun's ultraviolet rays. The atoms of chlorine that are freed destroy ozone molecules. Each atom of chlorine can destroy tens of thousands of ozone molecules.

But CFCs are not the only agent to destroy the ozone layer. The worst is methyl bromine, a pesticide widely used in developing countries, and forty times more dangerous than the CFCs.

20 The quantity of water vapour in the atmosphere has almost doubled since the beginning of the twentieth century. The causes of this increase are

not well known, even if one again suspects that it is due to human activity (increase in temperature, scorching of the biomass). This increase in water vapour affects the temperature in two different ways. On the one hand, it doubles the sensitivity of the climate to the increase in greenhouse gases, and therefore tends to raise the temperature. On the other hand, it forms a cloud cover which reflects sunlight and therefore reduces the amount of light reaching the ground. In this sense, it could slow the warming.

The influence of clouds on the greenhouse effect is not well understood — this is an important cause for uncertainty in atmospheric models.

Anthony D. Del Genio, "The dust settles on water vapour feedback," *Science*, vol. 296, 26 April 2002, p. 665–666.

21 The "brown cloud" over the Indian Ocean is a veil 3 kilometres thick made up of aerosol and pollutant soot. It continues to grow. It was discovered in 1996. It has been studied from satellites, balloons, and ships. According to *Science Magazine* (15 September 2002), quoting a NASA study, the dramatic floods in the south of China and the severe drought in the north of the country are due, at least in part, to the "brown cloud" made up of particles of soot that lies over the region.

22 *Nature*, 8 August 2002, p. 601.

Bibliography

A. Berger, *Le Climat de la Terre*, Brussels, De Boeckuniversité, 1992.

M.-L. Chanin, *European Review*, vol. 4, No. 2, p. 1.

O. E. Allen, *Atmosphere*, Alexandria VA, Time-Life Books, 1987.

Internet Sites

Official site of the Mission interministérielle de l'effet de serre, France: http://www.effet-de-serre.gouv.fr

Government of Canada Climate Change Site. (Act against climate change, Together we can prevail): http://www.climatechange.gc.ca

Météo France: http://www.meteo.fr/meteonet

Access to information on El Niño, on the site of the National Oceanic & Atmospheric Administration [NOAA], US Department of Commerce: http://www.pmel.noaa.gov/tao/elnino/nino-home.html

Site of the Agence de l'environnement et de la maîtrise de l'énergie, France: http://www.ademe.fr/htdocs/retad00.htm

2 *What Energies for Tomorrow?*

1 D. H. Meadows, D. L. Meadows, W. W. Behrens III, and J. Renders, *The Limits of Growth*, New York, Universe Books, 1972.

D. H. Meadows, D. L. Meadows, and J. Renders, *Beyond the Limits*, Post Mills, Chelsea Green Pub. Co., 1992.

2 Thorium can also be burned in slow neutron reactors. But its properties require the use of deuterium as a slowing agent (Canadian Candu type), easily used for making atomic bombs. That disqualifies this type of reactor on political grounds (Source: Yves Nifenaker, personal communication).

3 A British organization, the Oil Depletion Analysis Centre, presents detailed studies of all the planet's potential reserves, even those difficult to access today (underwater, polar, tarry, etc.). According to its conclusions, the production of conventional hydrocarbons (oil and gas) will start to decrease between 2010 and 2020, which implies a depletion before the end of the twenty-first century. Total reserves are estimated at between 2 and 4 trillion barrels.

R. W. Bentley, "Global oil and gas depletion: an overview," *Energy Policy*, No. 30, 2002, p. 189.

http://www.elsevier.com/locate/enpol

According to the article, "Advanced technology ..." (see bibliography below), accessible oil corresponds to 1,200 TWy, natural gas to 1,200 TWy, and coal to 4,800 TW. Divide by 14 TW (current consumption) or by 28 TW (predicted consumption for 2050) to estimate the date of depletion.

K. S. Deffeyes, *Hubbert's Peak: The Impending World Oil Shortage*, Princeton University Press, 2001 (*Scientific American*, October, 2001).

4 A report drawn up jointly by the Nuclear Energy Agency (NEA, an organ of the Organisation for Economic Co-operation and Development) and by the International Atomic Energy Agency (IAEA), and published in 1999, asserts that uranium resources recoverable at a reasonable cost amount to 4 million tonnes.

Higher estimates may be found in the article, "Advanced Technology ..." (see bibliography below). The range is from 4 to 17 million tonnes, or from 60 to 300 TWy. Here, as well, divide by 14 TW (current consumption) or by 28 TW (predicted consumption for 2050) to estimate the date of depletion.

5 The ocean's mass is about 1,018 tonnes, and within it the mass of oceanic uranium (3 grams per thousand tonnes of water) is 3 billion tonnes (3 Gt). To obtain the current annual global energy demand (12 TW) would require

the treatment of 6 million tonnes of water per second, or the equivalent flow of all the Earth's rivers towards the oceans, or 3,000 times the flow of the Rhône (1,700 m3 per second).

"Proceedings of the Fourth International Offshore and Polar Engineering Conference, Osaka," 10–15 April 1994.

6 The principle of the nuclear reactor is the following. We have several tonnes of uranium. Its atoms break down, giving off neutrons. These neutrons are captured by other uranium atoms, which themselves break down, generating other neutrons. These chain reactions produce energy, which we recover in the form of heat, to then be transformed into electricity.

Two sorts of uranium are present on Earth: uranium-238, which accounts for 99.3%, and uranium-235, which accounts for the remaining 0.7%. Current slow neutron reactors only use the latter. Fast neutron reactors use both. Plutonium-239 derives from the absorption of one neutron by one uranium-238. Like uranium-235, it has been used to make atomic bombs.

A nuclear reactor produces about 20 tonnes of waste per year, including about 200 kilograms of plutonium. The entire current nuclear industry (about five hundred reactors) generates 10,000 tonnes of waste, including 100 tonnes of plutonium.

It should be noted that for nuclear energy to make a significant contribution towards satisfying the demand for global energy, the number of reactors would have to be multiplied by twenty. The quantity of waste would then reach 200,000 tonnes, including 2,000 tonnes of plutonium.

7 The optimism of nuclear supporters is at times disarming. Here are the words of Richard Garwin, one of the world experts in nuclear problems: "Nuclear weapons proliferation is a grave risk [...] attached to deposition of nuclear waste in geological repository for effectively 100,000 years ... it will take constant and vigilant support by the United Nations International Energy Commission to insure that plutonium is not diverted to military purposes." (Source: Richard L. Garwin, "The Atom Option," *Newsweek*, 8–15 April 2002, p. 70–71.) "A vast program," as General de Gaulle would have said.

8 Super reactors are fast neutron reactors that have the advantage of being able to draw on all of natural uranium (U-235 and U-238) as their source of fuel, which increases a hundred times their potential reserves — these could then last several thousand more years. The high temperatures at which these generators function (more than 500°C) are the potential source of a number of problems. This has made the reactors extremely

unpopular, and has led to the shutting down of the French prototype (Super-Phénix). In the United States they are, up to now, prohibited due to the problems of waste and nuclear proliferation.

A few countries are continuing along this path (France, Russia, Japan) while banking on there being interesting innovations. The experts are skeptical. Considerable investment would be required to make these installations secure. And one would have to regain the confidence of the population, which is no small matter.

9 The solution of accelerator reactors (rubbiatrons) seems more promising. They function by bombarding heavy radioactive atoms (uranium, plutonium, and also thorium) with fluxes of fast protons to extract neutrons that produce the fission of heavy atoms, thereby generating energy.

Several laboratories are working on this actively, and could be operational within about thirty years. This solution would have the dual advantage of destroying the long-lasting nuclei, such as plutonium-239 (its longevity is the longest), and of generating energy. But it would not solve the problem of medium lifespan nuclei (which will remain active for several centuries), because they require secure stockpiling in their turn (though for a much shorter period of time). This solution appears to have been abandoned (2008).

10 Problems for countries that reprocess their waste, like France, will certainly be less serious, since the volume of waste to stockpile is less significant, and we foresee the possibility of transforming those types of waste with the longest radioactive periods. But, according to the French Commission for Sustainable Development, "the quantity of dangerous waste is only marginally reduced by the operation."

These countries will not be spared the need to bury waste for centuries, with all the risks and difficulties presently being encountered in the United States.

England is not immune to comparable problems (See: David Adam, "Public body appointed to clean up UK's nuclear legacy," *Nature*, vol. 418, 11 July 2002, p. 117).

11 For example, the total cost of the complete closing down of the Super-Phénix is estimated at 2.4 billion Euros.

12 "Chernobyl: an overlooked aspect," *Science*, 3 January 2002, p. 44.

13 "It is one of the major causes of worry to the Direction for the Security of Nuclear Installations (DSIN). Three-quarters of the incidents are, in fact, due to negligence and oversights. They are all the more frequent in that

the EDF sub-contracts to companies whose employees are less well-trained in radiation defence and the need for security."

14 James A. Lake, Ralph G. Bennett, and John F. Kotek, "Nuclear Power," *Scientific American*, January 2002, p. 71–79.

In the aftermath of the Soviet Union's collapse, 1,200 tonnes of highly enriched uranium were left vulnerable to theft by terrorist groups or governments wanting to develop nuclear weapons. Many co-operative programs financed by the United States have reduced the risk of this nuclear material being stolen. But much remains to be done, and Europe, which has expertise and resources, ought to be playing a more important role in dealing with this problem. (Source: *Euroscience News*, No. 21, Autumn, 2002 — see: http://www.euroscience.org.)

15 Regarding the cost of nuclear kWh, here are some typical texts, all written by experts. Judge for yourself.

First, the official advocates of nuclear energy:

- Jacques Bouchard: "These studies [by the Industry Ministry and the report of Mr. Charpin, Mr. Dessus, and Mr. Pellat] show that the nuclear kWh remains less costly [...]." (Source: J. Bouchard, *Le Monde*, 11 April 2002, p. 20.)
- Claude Mandil (Ministry of Industry): "The price of nuclear kWh is lower (0.65%) than that of coal. This price includes all the costs, from the construction of the generators to their dismantling, plus their operation (stockpiling of the wastes, and security)."

Then the others:

- Amory Lowins, founder of the Rocky Mountain Institute, an American research and consulting organization for energy (http://www.rmi.org): "Nuclear energy has shown itself to be more costly than predicted; much more costly, in fact, than all other ways of producing electricity. Governments would be well-advised to respect the laws of the marketplace rather than giving priority to this technology at the expense of the taxpayer."
- Bruno Barillot: "The price per kWh is the least expensive in Europe if one overlooks the hidden costs paid by all Frenchmen, even if they're not visible on the electricity bill. The costs of dismantling have always been underestimated by electricity producers, and the total cost of dealing with the waste remains unknown. Tomorrow, we and our descendants will still be paying for these nuclear kWh that have already been consumed."

- *Scientific American*, January 2002: "Far from producing energy at a negligible cost, the reactors have been the most expensive energy option. To be economically viable, the new projects would have to cost less than 1,000 dollars per electric kW. Some projects will cost three times that."
- "No one has the slightest idea of the costs involved in the nuclear industry, or the expenditures that will be required for the dismantling of the reactors and the managing of the nuclear wastes." (Source: *New Scientist*, 25 August 2001, p. 3. Cited in the scientific press review of CERN, *Picked Up For You*, 2000–2015, p. 4.)

16 "Nuclear revival? Even the safest reactors will still make accountants sweat," *New Scientist*, 25 August 2001, p. 3 (editorial). (Source: Scientific press review for CERN, *Picked Up For You*, 2000–2015, p. 4.)

"Is nuclear power ready?" (editorial), *Scientific American*, January 2002.

James A. Lake, Ralph G. Benett, and John F. Kotek, "Nuclear Power," *Scientific American*, January 2002, p. 71–79.

"Revising nuclear power safety plant," *Science*, 10 January 2003, p. 201.

Martin Durrani, "New design on nuclear energy," *Physics World*, July 2002, p. 42.

17 "Wind energy growth continues," *Vital Signs*, 2001, p. 44.

A windmill of 1,000 kW, under normal conditions, spares us an annual discharge equivalent to 2,000 tonnes of carbon dioxide from coal generators. (Source: *Scientific American*, March 2002.)

Mark Fischetti, "Windmills," *Scientific American*, July 2002, p. 70–71.

W. Williams, "Blowing out to sea," *Scientific American*, March 2002.

18 The European Union wants to encourage biofuels. In years to come, yellow fields of colza may well be carpeting even more of the countryside. But there are numerous problems associated with this operation.

19 "Solar power market surge," *Vital Signs*, 2001.

Pierre Bec, "The sun in batteries — Renewable energy: at the urging of *Genec*, a European network is being set up to explore the various technologies for stockpiling solar energy," *Les Défis du CEA*, May–June 2002, p. 33.

The system of solar panels is based on the photovoltaic effect discovered by Edmond Becquerel in 1839. When photons strike certain materials, such as silicon, they transfer their energy to electrons that circulate in the metal, and that can generate differences in potential. Used in 1958 by the Vanguard 1 space satellite, these solar panels raised a lot of hopes, but also caused disappointment due to technical difficulties. Despite significant progress over the last twenty years (with an efficiency of over 30% in some cases), the installation cost remains high in relation to the output. More technical progress will still be necessary.

Bibliography

I. Fells, "The need for energy," *Europhysics News*, November 1998.

R. L. Garwin and G. Charpak, *Megawatts and Megatons*, New York, Knopf, 2001.

J. Goldenberg (under the direction of), *World Energy Assessment*, New York, ONU, 2001.

P. Hofman, *Tomorrow's Energy: Hydrogen, Fuel Cells and the Prospects for a Cleaner Planet*, Cambridge, MIT Press, 2001.

M. I. Offert, "Advanced technology paths to global climate stability: energy for a greenhouse planet," *Science*, 1 November 2002.

"Energy challenges for the 21st century," *Physics World*, July 2002.

"Nevada takes nuclear waste to court," *Nature*, vol. 415, 3 January 2002, p. 6.

Nature, 30 August 2002.

Physics World, July 2001.

Internet Sites

Nuclear Energy Agency, OECD: http://www.nea.fr

The French nuclear industry and material sites; it would seem to be an Icelandic site: http://www.francenuc.org

Worldwatch Institute: http://www.worldwatch.org

English sites dealing exclusively with Chernobyl: http://www.chernobyl. co.uk and http://www.chernobyl.com

3 *What Are We Going to Eat Tonight?*

1 "The end of world population growth," *Nature*, vol. 412, 2 August 2001, p. 543–545. (Source: Scientific press review of CERN, *Picked Up For You*, 2000–2015.)

See also: Nico Keilman, "Uncertain population forecasts," *Nature*, vol. 412, 2 August 2001, p. 490–491; "Population growing steadily," *Vital Signs*, 2002, p. 88.

2 "World grains harvests lagging behind demand," Worldwatch Institute, *Vital Signs*, 2002, p. 26.

"Grain area declines," *Vital Signs*, 1999, p. 42.

"Farmland quality deteriorating," *Vital Signs*, 2002, p. 102.

David S. Reay, "Intensive farming, US-style, is not sustainable worldwide — more greenhouse gases will increase loss of usable land," *Nature*, vol. 417, 2 May 2002, p. 15.

3 Peter Raven, *Nature*, 31 August 2001.

4 "The other global pollutant: nitrogen proves tough to curb," *Science*, vol. 294, 9 November 2001, p. 1268.

5 "Pesticide sales remain strong," *Vital Signs*, 2002, p. 126.

6 According to a study published by the Arctic Monitoring and Assessment Programme (AMAP), the native populations of the Arctic, especially the Inuit, are threatened by the increasing presence of toxins of human origin in a region that had been relatively pollution-free. (Source: AFP, October 2002.)

7 The world catch of fish was five million tonnes per year at the end of the nineteenth century. It reached eighty-six million tonnes at the end of the 1990s.

"Fisheries falter," *Vital Signs*, 1999, p. 36.

"Low stocks prompt call for North Atlantic fishing ban," *Nature*, October 2002, p. 886.

We are now exploiting the three major sources of marine protein that are still abundant: Antarctic shrimp, the squid of the great oceans, and organisms of extreme depths.

Ten years after the ban on cod fishing, the stocks have still not replenished themselves in Canadian waters.

"How many more fish in the sea?" *Nature*, 17 October 2002, p. 662.

8 "Freshwater species at increasing risks," *Vital Signs*, 2002, p. 106.

9 "Aquaculture production intensifies," *Vital Signs*, 2002, p. 24.

Farming, which represents 30% of fishing, is done in large part with cereals. And so it does not add a great deal to food production.

10 We must remember that water is an element that is essential to life. It exists on Earth in three forms: gas (water vapour), liquid, and solid. We must then make a distinction between the salt water in the seas (which represents more than 97% of liquid water), and fresh water that humans can use. Most of this fresh water is imprisoned in glaciers, primarily on the continent of Antarctica (2.15%), with surface water representing only 0.015%, and subterranean water representing only 0.635% — with these sources constituting the bulk of our accessible fresh water. And so,

drinkable fresh water represents about 2.5% of the water on the planet, and less than 1% of this water is accessible.

11 This study recommends public programs for economizing water, incentives for farmers, encouraging them to modernize their irrigation systems, and active participation from the private sector.

The International Programme for Technology and Research in Irrigation & Drainage: Food and Agriculture Organization of the United Nations (FAO).

http://www.fao.org/iptrid/kn_syn_04/kn_syn_04.htm

12 The discharge of nitrates into the ocean environment (via waterways) has almost doubled in France since 1985, although it ought to have been reduced by half according to international conventions for the protection of marine environments. "Towards lake eutrophication, from phosphates and detergents," *Science*, 27 September 2002, p. 220.

13 Quirin Schiermeier, "Ecologists plot to turn the tide for shrinking lake," *Nature*, vol. 412, 23 August 2001, p. 756.

14 "Wetlands decline," *Vital Signs*, 2001, p. 96.

15 Food and Agriculture Organization (FAO), 2001 Rome report.

"Forest loss unchecked," *Vital Signs*, 2002, p. 104.

16 Between 1995 and 2000, the destruction of the Brazilian Amazon has risen to the same level as during the years 1970–1980: 1.9 million hectares per year, or seven football fields per minute, according to a study conducted recently from satellite photos by the National Institute of Amazon Research.

17 Hundreds of starving monkeys have pillaged plantations and devoured tonnes of bananas in the west of the Indonesian island of Java, after having been driven from their natural habitat by deforestation. (Source: AFP, 17 September 2002.)

Constance Holden, "World's richest forest in peril," *Science*, vol. 295, 8 February 2002, p. 963.

18 A study conducted in Switzerland comparing organic to traditional agriculture over twenty years has shown that fertility is 40% greater in soil cultivated organically compared to soil exploited intensively with chemical fertilizer, and 85% greater than soil exploited in the conventional fashion. http://www.biogene.org/e/themen/biotech/e-news17.htm

19 According to a report by the French Institute for the Environment (May 2002), we are seeing a deterioration of natural environments due to pollu-

tion that continues to worsen. Road transport of merchandise, for example, has gone from a rate of growth below 2% in 1997, to 3.5% in 1998, then to 6% in 1999. Certainly, technological measures (catalytic converters ...) have put a brake on atmospheric pollution, but this progress has been wiped out by an increase in traffic. Also, the quantity of waste products continues to grow at the same pace as consumption. The report notes this with some severity: "The major problems facing us today remain much like those that were already plaguing us at the beginning of the 1990s: questions linked to agriculture and nourishment, the problem of waste and the exponential growth in the transport sector, whose impact on greenhouse gas emissions continues to grow." Successive governments have been powerless to control the impact of intensive agriculture on the soil, the quality of our water, and biodiversity. For example, the number of sites affected by the "green tide" phenomena on the coastlines of Brittany (a proliferation of algae due to nitrates) has virtually doubled since 1997. The state was, in fact, censured on 8 March 2001 by the Court of Justice of the European Community for not having protected the quality of water in Brittany. What this document indicates is that the return of economic growth in France between 1998 and 2001 was accompanied by a deterioration of the environment, which shows that "economic growth" and "respect for the environment" do not harmonize. (Source: *Le Monde*, May 2002.)

20 "Hostilities resume over future of GM crops," *Nature*, September 2002, p. 327.

21 "'The biggest risk of developing genetically modified (GM) animals is that they might alter the environments,' according to a new report from the National Research Council [of the United States]." (Source: Eric Stokstad, "Environmental impact seen as biggest risk," *Science*, 23 August 2002, p. 1257; http://www.sciencemag.org.)

"Pesticide-resistant species flourish" and "OGM threatens to exasperate resistance trends," *Vital Signs*, 1999, p. 124 and 125.

"Engineered fish: friend or foe of the environment," *Science*, 13 September 2002, p. 1797.

Bibliography

Direction De L'Industrie, *Les Pratiques des gestions polluées en France. Connaître pour agir*, Paris, Ademe éditions, 2001.

R. Dumont, *Famines, le retour*, Paris, Politis-Arléa, 1997.

Internet Sites
The International Programme for Technology & Research in Irrigation & Drainage, on the site of the Food and Agriculture Organization [FAO] of the United Nations: http://www.fao.org/iptrid/kn_syn_04/kn_syn_04.htm

4 *A Soiled Planet: The Augean Stables*

1 Daniel Lovering, "Killing Fields of Laos," *Scientific American*, August 2001, p. 57–61.

The eradication of anti-personnel mines has accelerated considerably since the treaty banning mines was signed in Ottawa in December 1997. But India and Pakistan are laying mines in great numbers all along their borders. (Source: *Politis*, 19 September 2002.)

http://www.handicap-international.org
http://www.landmines.org

2 "A chemical weapons atlas," *The Bulletin of the Atomic Scientist*, September–October 1997.

Educational Foundation for Nuclear Science: http://www.bullatomsci.org

Site for documentation on chemical weapons: http://www.multimania.com/armch/

Biological arsenals: "Timetable for talks keeps hopes alive on bioweapons treaty (Biological and Toxin Weapons Convention, 1972)," *Nature*, 21 November 2002, p. 259.

3 Richard Stone, "Down to the wire on bioweapons talks," *Science*, vol. 293, 20 July 2001, p. 416.

"How not to make friends," *Nature*, vol. 412, 2 August 2001, p. 463.

Nature, 13 December 2001.

4 Sites dealing with armaments in general:

http://www.alsapresse.com/jdj/99/08/12/MA/article_1.html
http://obsarm.org
http://www.stratisc.org

5 "Global nuclear stockpiles 1945–2002," *The Bulletin of the Atomic Scientist*, November–December 2002, p. 123.

More than 128,000 nuclear warheads have been built. There remain about 20,000, with 10,600 in the United States, 8,600 in Russia, 200 in the United Kingdom, 350 in France, 400 in China, fewer than 200 in India and Pakistan, and 200 (unofficial estimate) in Israel.

6 "Nuclear arsenals shrink," *Vital Signs*, 1999, p. 116.
"Limited progress on nuclear arsenals," *Vital Signs*, 2001, p. 86.

7 Gordon Thompson, "Checks on the spread," *Nature*, vol. 318, 14 November 1985, p. 127–128.
http://www.un.org/News/fr-press/docs/2001/AGDSI274.doc.htm

8 Norway is going to help Russia finance the reprocessing of the fuel for its nuclear icebreakers preserved for years in a floating sarcophagus at Murmansk, a Russian port on the Barents Sea (northwest). Also, the risk capital company NEFCO (Nordic Environment Finance Corporation) has committed itself to contributing 1.3 million Euros to the project, according to the same source. NEFCO, which includes Denmark, Finland, Iceland, Norway, and Sweden, has as its mandate the financing of environmental projects in Eastern and Central Europe. (Source: AFP, 24 September 2002.)

9 http://www.hanford.gov

10 http://home.breathenet.de/user/gilles.vibert/1970/I1970_3.htm

11 "Toxic waste largely unseen," *Vital Signs*, 2002, p. 112.

12 Rebecca Renner, "A case of the vapors — Ground toxins diffusing into homes prove hard to assess," *Scientific American*, July 2002, p. 13.

13 T. D. Beamish, *Silent Spill: The Organization of Industrial Crisis*, Cambridge, MIT Press, 2002.
Paul Schulman, "Lessons from a slow leak," *Science*, vol. 296, 24 May 2002, p. 1403–1404.
From 1948 to 1990, a hundred thousand tonnes of toxic diluents were injected into oil wells at Guadalupe Dunes, north of Los Angeles, to dilute the oil, which was too viscous.

14 "PVC plastics pervade economy," *Vital Signs*, 2001, p. 108.

15 "Invasion by marine life on plastic debris," *Nature*, 25 April 2002, p. 416.

16 R. Crowther, "Space-junk — Protecting space for future generations," *Science*, 17 May 2002, p. 1241.

17 "Blinded by the light"
http://www.lightpollution.it/dmsp
"Save starry night," *Nature*, vol. 418, 15 August 2002, p. 709.
An association: The International Dark Sky Association.

Bibliography

J. Lederberg, *Biological Weapons: Limiting the Threat*, Cambridge, MIT Press, 1999.

5 *The Animals, Our Brothers*

1 Genesis 1: 26–30.

2 A. Balmford, et al., "Economic reasons for conserving wild nature," *Science*, vol. 297, 9 August 2002, p. 950–953.

3 "How many species revisited," *Biological Journal Soc.*, 73, 279, 2001.

http://www.all-species.org. The authors of this site have undertaken, on a scale of twenty-five years, to classify the entire living world: animal, vegetable, and bacterial.

"Estimating the size of the world's threatened flora," *Science*, 1 November 2002, p. 989.

4 P. Brunel, "Marine biodiversity," Unesco, 2002.

Encyclopedia of Life Support Systems, p. 1.

5 Gilbert Chin (under the direction of), "How many species, revisited," *Science*, vol. 295, 8 March 2002, p. 1835.

6 "A global experiment under way — Habitat loss and fragmentation are the principal factors of biodiversity loss, notably in the tropics," *Science*, vol. 295, 8 March 2002, p. 1835.

7 "Bird species threatened," *Vital Signs*, 2001, p. 98.

8 Washington Convention on Endangered Species, CITES: http://www.cites.org.

9 "Lions in trouble," *Science*, vol. 294, 9 November 2001, p. 1275.

"Lions in peril — The future looks bleak for Africa's big cats," *New Scientist*, 3 November 2001, p. 7.

10 According to a study by the Churchill Northern Studies Centre (CNSC) in Manitoba, Canada, the population of polar bears around Hudson Bay, estimated at more than a thousand, is in great danger. "In twenty years, the date for the ice breakup in Hudson Bay has advanced on average by two weeks," and in autumn the ice forms a week and a half later. Polar bears need the ice to feed themselves, hunting ringed or bearded seals on the pack ice. "A week less hunting on the ice deprives the bear of 10 kilos of fat in reserve," an essential factor in its survival for the five summer and autumn months when it must fast.

11 http://bonoboducongo.free.fr

12 During the meeting of the International Whaling Commission in 2002, and despite the considerable pressure exerted by the hunting countries led by Japan, no extra privileges were accorded them.

Mexico has just created a sea refuge of three million square kilometres (six times the area of France) to protect the whales (Source: Letter from the Mexican ambassador to ROC, 22 July 2002) (http://www.roc.asso.fr).

13 On November 15, 2002, the Maui County Council, in Hawaii, voted unanimously to prohibit the display of whales and dolphins in captivity.

14 The Atlantic salmon passes its first years in the river, and then makes its way to Greenland; it then returns to its native river.

Because of dams, pollution, and overfishing, this population has decreased by 78% in recent years. In France, it has totally disappeared from certain waters (The Dordogne, Garonne, Meuse, Moselle, Seine, Tarn). But, and this is good news, thanks to programs designed to reintroduce the species, it can today be found in the Loire, the Rhine, and the Elbe. (Source: Prague, AFP, 1 November 2002.)

15 The proportion of severely damaged coral in the world has risen from 10% in 1992 to 27% in 2000. It is seriously affected by human activity: fishing with dynamite, harvesting for aquariums.

When the water temperature rises by a single degree, during events such as El Niño, microscopic organisms that live in symbiosis with the coral are expelled, and the coral turns white.

"World's coral reefs dying off," *Vital Signs*, 2001, p. 92.

"Survey confirms coral reefs are in peril," *Science*, 6 September 2002, p. 1622.

"Coral campaign gets massive funding boost," *Nature*, vol. 410, 22 March 2001, p. 402.

16 The number of sea horses has decreased considerably in recent years due to their overfishing. Catches increased from 25 to 75% between 1990 and 1995 in countries where they are principally commercialized (India, Indonesia, Thailand, and the Philippines). The sea horse is used in traditional medicine, sold dried as a curio, and live for aquariums.

17 Constance Holden (under the direction of), "Ocean Rx," *Science*, vol. 295, 8 March 2002, p. 1827.

Tortoises, mainly in Asia, have in recent years seen their numbers diminish to a disturbing degree because of unbridled commercial exploitation and illegal captures. Some are particularly prized as food products or for their medicinal properties, others as pets. The largest territory in the world for their egg-laying, on the beaches of Malaysia, has shrunk by 99%.

According to Eric Niller ("The trouble with turtles," *Scientific American*, January 2002, p. 71–75), the tortoises of Baja, California, have been reduced in number from 1,290 in 1990 to 145 in 2000.

Several dozens of sea turtles have died off the French coasts, primarily from the ingestion of plastic waste. (Source: http://www.wwf.fr.)

Twenty-six species of tortoises, for the most part in danger of extinction, have been included in Appendix 2 ("Controlled commercialization") of CITES.

18 In 1860, the Sierra Club in the United States was the first NGO for the defence of nature, and in 1872, Yellowstone Park became the first great governmental nature park.

19 Seventy-one cows were recently slaughtered due to ingesting lead bullets that came from a nearby trap shooting range.

20 A survey of 2000 children showed that 16.5% of boys and 4.5% of girls had participated in a hunting expedition. Only 11.5% of all these children said they enjoyed hunting.

21 *Animal People*, May 2002.

22 Recognizing the cruelty with which animals (foxes, hares) were killed and dismembered by the jaws of trained dogs, the members of the Scottish Parliament voted on February 14, 2002, against such hunting. (Source: International Fund for Animal Welfare, February 2002.)

23 Greenland: http://cphpost.periskop.dk/default.asp?id=19095

24 On May 17, 2002, the German Parliament unanimously declared itself in favour of better animal protection. "The State takes the responsibility for protecting the normal conditions of life for animals, in the interests of future generations."

On April 22, 2002, the National Criminal Intelligence Service (NCIS) was created in Britain to combat organized crime as it affects wild animals, both at the national and international levels.

25 In Italy, a survey conducted for the League for the Abolition of the Hunting of Small Birds showed that 87% of people questioned were opposed to this form of hunting.

26 See, in this connection, the Universal Declaration of Animal Rights, a text with no legal authority, but which commands attention.

Internet Site

Site of *Science Magazine*, in the United States, published by The American Association for the Advancement of Science with the assistance of Stanford University's Highwise Press: http://www.sciencemag.org

6 *The Spectre of Planetary Poverty*

1 In 2002, The FAO Congress set the number of people suffering from malnutrition at eight hundred and fifteen million.

"Hydrological poverty worsening: one-fifth of humanity has no access to a safe water supply and two-fifths has inadequate sanitation," *Vital Signs*, 2001, p. 94.

2 Ismail Serageldin, "World poverty and hunger — the challenge for science," *Science*, vol. 296, 5 April 2002, p. 54–58.

"Poor to feel pinch of rising fish prices," *Science*, 8 November 2002, p. 1154.

3 "Refuges migrant and refugees on the move," *Vital Signs*, p. 142.

New Zealand is preparing to welcome 11,000 inhabitants of the Tuvalu Islands because of the rising sea levels. Also at risk are the Kiribati archipelago (300,000 inhabitants) and the famous Falkland Islands, a touristic jewel.

4 Bjørn Lomborg, *The Skeptical Environmentalist. Measuring the Real Estate of the World*, Cambridge, Cambridge University Press, 2001.

5 According to the World Health Organization, only 5% of the money spent on biomedical research targets diseases affecting 95% of impoverished people.

6 "AIDS erodes decades of progress," *Vital Signs*, 2001.

7 About forty-five years instead of sixty-seven years on average, and falling since 1990; see "Life expectancy in Africa," *Vital Signs*, 1999, p. 100.

8 The zeal with which certain religious groups, to the highest reaches of their power structure, continue to defend their stand on family planning is one of the sources of our global "unending underdevelopment."

9 May 2002: The United Nations Environment Programme publishes its "Third report on the future of the global environment."

10 An average of 40% in poor countries; in sub-Saharan Africa, 80% of their national product. Two thousand billion dollars, or 300 dollars per person (Source: *Vital Signs*, 1999, p. 66).

"Third world debt still rising," *Vital Signs*, 1999, p. 66.

11 "Foreign aid spending falls," *Vital Signs*, 2002, p. 118 (0.22% GNP).

7 *Taking Action*

1 In June of 1923, an international conference on ecology took place at the National Museum of Natural History in Paris. The most significant progress

achieved between the two sides was made, above all, by the ornithologists, beginning with the creation of the International Committee for the Protection of Birds in London in June of 1922.

North American countries drew up a treaty on migratory birds in 1937, and an Inter-American Convention for the protection of flora, fauna, and natural panoramic beauty in 1940. Most large global associations for the protection of the environment, like Greenpeace or the WWF, saw the light of day between 1960 and 1970.

2 A few important dates:

- June 1972: A declaration by the World Conference on the Human Environment in Stockholm aims to protect nature for future generations;
- 1984: The UN creates the World Commission of Environment and Development, headed by the Norwegian, Gro Harlem Bruntland. Her report appears in 1987;
- August 1987: Governments sign the Montreal Protocol for the protection of the ozone layer. It is applied in 1989;
- June 1992: The Earth Summit takes place at Rio de Janeiro;
- June 1994: Governments sign the convention to combat desertification at UNESCO Headquarters in Paris;
- December 1997: The Kyoto Conference on climate change. A protocol on the reduction in greenhouse gases;
- 2000: The Carthagena Protocol (Spain), on the prevention of technological risk-taking, is adopted;
- August 2002: the Earth Summit in Johannesburg.

3 The Rio Protocol imposed a 6% reduction in carbon dioxide emissions across the world. It was a very modest step, given the UN report establishing that climate stabilization would require a reduction of 60 to 80%. In fact, a global increase of 9% was recorded between 1992 and 2001 (18% in the United States), with, what is more, an abandonment of the protocol by the United States, responsible on its own for 24% of global emissions. Given the extremely important problem of water management, Rio created "Agenda 21" to deal with the use of water resources, emphasizing in particular the supply of water to poor countries. The Rio resolutions looked ahead to a major reduction in mortality from diarrhea and measles. Progress was made, but it fell far short of expectations.

4 "Global Environment Outlook-3," the report of the United Nations Environment Programme (May 22, 2002), does not contain only bad news:

- In ten years, eight hundred million people have benefited from a better supply of water;
- Today, protected territories are five times as extensive as they were ten years ago;
- A moratorium on whaling has enabled a number of species to recover.

5 In Canada, the deterioration of the Great Lakes sounded the alarm at the end of the 1960s. Far too many phosphates were accumulating in the water. The federal government adopted, in 1972, a law limiting the presence of phosphates in detergents to 5%.

6 To combat smog, which usually only forms over 25°C, the city of Chicago decided to place two thousand plants on the roof of its City Hall. Result: a 5°C lowering of the local temperature.

Toronto City Hall has targeted the city's rooftops to make them oases of greenery, in order to combat pollution and heat waves, which are increasingly long and frequent during the summer. (Source: AFP, 30 October 2002.)

In this regard, we can also cite the efforts of Bertrand Delanoë, Mayor of Paris.

7 Ramsar sites: http://www.detr.gov.uk

8 These initiatives, however, often did no more than to transfer the problem to other countries. China and the Philippines favour the importation of wood to the detriment of neighbouring countries such as Cambodia, Indonesia, Burma, and Russia.

C. Brown, P. Durst, and T. Enters, "Effectiveness of logging bans in natural forest in Asia-Pacific," FAO.

9 http://www.futura-sciences.com/news550.php

10 The population of groupers has increased considerably in the protected waters of Port-Cros, one of the islands of Hyères. In 1973, a dozen groupers were counted in the south of the island. Twenty years later, eighty-five of these fish were seen near Port-Cros; there were about 300 in 1999.

11 An article in the *Wall Street Journal* recounts that in the west of Texas a fleet of trucks transported, day after day, 550,000 pines that were used to reforest part of the fallow prairie. The project, which cost the equivalent of 2.8 million Euros, was financed in its entirety by a Franco-Italian multinational.

12 The BioCoop network is a federation of over 200 independent consumer co-operatives and shops in France (and now with members in Portugal and Spain) who share ideals, objectives, and structures. Its goals: "For an

agriculture respectful of the environment, that protects the soil, that consumes little fossil energy, that uses no synthetic chemical products, that preserves resources for the long term, that is a source of health for mankind, that creates employment in a sector that is in difficulty.

Through producer-consumer relations based on solidarity, and respect for the interests and needs of each.

Through a social policy grounded in responsibility and fellowship.

Through an active participation in regional and national initiatives of organic agriculture.

Through commercial relations with third-world countries that do not aggravate their underdevelopment and assure their autonomy.

Through the transparency of targeted goals, of the rules of procedure, and the results obtained, in order to maintain a climate of confidence among all the partners.

By a sensitization to the realities of production and distribution, leading to an ecological approach."

13 "Bangladesh's poisoned wells — Scientists and government officials bear collective responsibility for an unfolding tragedy," *Nature*, vol. 413, 11 October 2001, p. 551.

14 "Brazil and the World Bank have signed an agreement, outside the Earth Summit, that would triple the protected area of the Amazonian forest. The protected zone has been increased to 50 million hectares, representing 3.6% of the world's tropical forest.

With 5.5 million square kilometres, the Amazonian territory covers more than 60% of Brazil, or the equivalent of Western Europe." (Source: Johannesburg, AFP, 3 September 2002.)

The Madagascan authorities are prepared to issue a decree banning all exploitation and export of wood for six months. The motive: unscrupulous economic operators are exporting precious wood at a great rate.

15 More aggressive measures, such as the creation of a specialized police force, must be adopted to control the illegal trade of animals and plants in danger of extinction, declared a highly-placed representative of CITES, whose twelfth conference took place in Santiago. (Source: *Santiago*, vol. 293, 31 August 2001, p. 1579–1580.)

16 Site for equitable trade: http://www.commerceequitable.org. Artisans of the World: http://www.artisansdumonde.org. Artisans of the World is a grouping of co-operatives, suppliers, and distributors.

17 Here are the most urgent measures to be taken, according to Mikhaïl

Gorbachev, today founder and former president of Green Cross International, an NGO created in 1993 following the Rio summit:

- to reform the UN and endow it with real executive power to enforce its decisions;
- to ratify without delay the protocols relevant to disarmament, the banning of weapons, a reduction in greenhouse gases, the safeguarding of biodiversity, and access to water;
- to reduce the debt of poor countries;
- to, from the very beginning, make environmental preservation part and parcel of all plans for economic development.

18 All of them close to hand. Do not leave household appliances running, use light bulbs that save energy, choose organic products and garden as much as possible, limit automobile travel, buy vehicles that consume little fuel, and reduce speed.

We must create, as soon as possible, an international agreement, modelled on the Kyoto Agreement, to limit the manufacture of gas-guzzling automobiles. Today, we are producing perfectly functional cars that burn barely 3 litres per 100 kilometres, while the average on our roads is 12 litres per 100 kilometres. And we must tax more heavily fuel expenses associated with leisure (automobile races, pleasure trips ...). We could, for example, as with cigarettes, demand that advertisements for cars state: "The overconsumption of fuel is a threat to the planet."

We can also favour products that respect the environment, only wear synthetic fur, limit the use of plastic bags, insulate our homes effectively ... All these are individual initiatives that, together, can make a significant difference.

Plants in danger: a large proportion of threatened plants are found in regions of highly concentrated population (vacant lots, municipal gardens). Coordinated efforts could be made to gather information from botanists, to uproot undesirable plants that could harm them, to evaluate what is there, to coordinate the gathering and storing of the plants. (Source: M. W. Schwartz, N. Jurjavcic, and J. O'Brien, "You can help rare plants survive in the cities," *Nature*, vol. 411, 28 June 2001, p. 991–992.)

Respect the ecosystems: by removing too much dead wood in our gardens and forests, we place a number of ecosystems in danger. Rotting wood plays a crucial role on Earth and in water. It triggers sequences of biotic interaction and represents a nourishing oasis. Dead trees are the home, first, of mushrooms, bacteria, and worms, then woodpeckers, titmice, bluebirds, and squirrels. Martens and bats takeover nests abandoned by the woodpeckers. When foresters "clean out" the undergrowth, the owls and salmon (which used the smell of wood rotting in water) are endangered. (Source: "Defending dead wood," *Science*, 31 August 2001.)

Discussion group: http://www.egroups.com/group/dead_wood

19 Many organizations exist that have taken concrete action. Here are a few addresses:

France Nature Environnement: http://www.fne.asso.fr. France Nature Environnement is a federation that includes more than 3000 associations.

League for the Preservation of Wild Animals: http://www.roc.asso.fr

World Wildlife Fund: http://www.wwf.org

Greenpeace: http://www.greenpeace.org

Eau Secours! Canada: http://www.eausecours.org

Americana, the environmental technology trade show for the Americas: http://www.americana.org

ABOUT THE AUTHOR

HUBERT REEVES WAS BORN IN Montreal and resides in France where he is the Director of Research at the Centre National de la Recherche Scientifique. He is also a well-known popularizer of science and appears frequently on French television. He has written many bestselling books in France, including *Atoms of Silence* and *The Hour of Our Delight*.